KURSK

KURSK

THE WORLD'S GREATEST TANK BATTLE

RUPERT MATTHEWS

ARCTURUS

ARCTURUS

This edition published in 2016 by Arcturus Publishing Limited
26/27 Bickels Yard, 151–153 Bermondsey Street,
London SE1 3HA

Typesetting by Palimpsest Book Production Limited

ISBN: 978-1-78599-384-8
DA004728UK

Printed in China

Contents

STALINGRAD

The war between Germany and the Soviet Union had begun in June 1941. A vast German army, supported by Finnish, Hungarian, Slovak and Italian allies, surged into the Soviet Union. It was one of the largest and most complex military operations ever mounted, with 3.8 million men taking part.

The war was driven by the ideology of the German dictator Adolf Hitler and the Nazi Party that he led. The Nazis held that the Germanic peoples were superior to all other races and nations; the Slavonic peoples of the east were their inferiors. Ultimately the Nazis aimed to reduce the Slavs to servile status, little better than slaves working for German settlers who would be moved into the conquered territories in large numbers. Even without the planned extermination of the Jews, the Nazi plans meant that conquered populations had much to fear from German occupation.

Hitler had planned to defeat the Soviet Union in the first year of campaigning – repeating his swift conquests of Poland, France and other countries, which had all fallen after just a few weeks of fighting. It was to be *blitzkrieg* – 'lightning war' – on an epic scale.

At first all seemed to go well for the Germans. Their columns of armoured panzers, supported by infantry riding in trucks, struck deep and far into Soviet territory. Behind the advancing panzer spearheads, German infantry mopped up the disorientated and disrupted Soviet armies. Within a few months the Soviets had lost 4 million men killed or wounded and another 4 million captured. German tanks were in the suburbs of Moscow and vast areas of the western Soviet Union were under German control.

Despite these stunning successes, the Germans had not won the war by the end of 1941. The Soviets had been able to mobilize far more men, tanks and aircraft than the Germans had thought possible. The invaders had defeated far more armies than they had expected to encounter, and yet still the Soviets would not surrender.

A fresh assault

In 1942 Hitler decided to try again. This time the main thrust of the German attack would be in the south. A new German offensive was to capture the vast wheatfields, coalfields and oilfields of the southern steppes, then push on to the Caspian Sea and capture the lower reaches of the River Volga. That would deprive the Soviets of many of the raw materials that they needed to produce weapons. It would also place the German army in a position to launch a massive strike north in 1943 up the Volga and Don rivers to capture the Russian heartlands and outflank their armies.

Opposite: Hitler studies a map of the Kursk area at the headquarters of Manstein's Army Group South. To his right are Richard Ruoff (17th Army commander) and Manstein, while to his left are Kurt Zeitzler (Chief of Staff), von Kleist (Army Group A), Werner Kempf (Army Detachment Kempf) and Wolfram von Richthofen (Luftwaffe).

Things did not turn out as Hitler had planned. Instead of concentrating on the main objectives, he allowed himself to get sucked into a murderous battle for the secondary objective of the city of Stalingrad, situated on the lower Volga. The tank/bomber combination at which the Germans excelled was almost useless in urban fighting, so Stalingrad allowed the Soviets to face the Germans on equal terms for the first time. The result was catastrophe for the Germans. By the opening days of January 1943 the entire German 6th Army was surrounded in Stalingrad, while the remaining German forces in the south were hurrying back in retreat to avoid a similar fate.

Things appeared to be bleak for the Germans. And yet the German war machine had a remarkable capacity to recover from hammer blows such as Stalingrad. Victory was still attainable, and 1943 was going to be the year when that victory would become assured – or so Hitler planned.

Chapter 1

THE CITADEL

The planning for what was to become the German Operation *Zitadelle* (Citadel), the Battle of Kursk, was long in coming and slow in formation. It grew out of a desire to do something on the Eastern Front, combined with the knowledge that the losses at Stalingrad meant that a major war-winning offensive was impossible.

In part the disastrous decision to launch the Battle of Kursk grew out of the increasingly confused German command structure, combined with the personalities of the men involved. In theory the German High Command had a clear and relatively simple structure.

Command structure

At the top was Adolf Hitler himself as Führer and supreme warlord of Germany. Hitler, however, was also the head of the government of Germany, so in practice the command of the armed forces was in the hands of military professionals. At first Hitler merely took an interest and sometimes overruled the professionals, but as the years passed his involvement grew rapidly.

The top organization in the German armed forces was the *Oberkommando der Wehrmacht* (Supreme Command of the

Armed Forces), usually termed OKW. This was the overall strategic planning body that made the big overview decisions, allocated resources between the army, air force and navy, and liaised with the suppliers and manufacturers who designed and produced weaponry.

The chief of OKW was Field Marshal Wilhelm Keitel, who had taken over the post in 1939 and would hold it until 1945. Keitel was a successful and talented career army officer, though some of his colleagues suspected that his elevation to the supreme command in 1939 had more to do with his admiration for Hitler than his military skills.

Under OKW were the supreme command bodies of the army, air force and navy. The body commanding the army was *Oberkommando des Heeres*, or OKH. In 1939 the OKH was led by another talented career officer – Walther von Brauchitsch. Brauchitsch oversaw the German army during the Polish and French campaigns, and the early months of the Russian war. However, in November 1941 he suffered a heart attack, which made him an ideal scapegoat for the failure to capture Moscow. Hitler sacked Brauchitsch, then took the unprecedented step of assuming the position of head of OKH himself.

This created the anomalous situation in which Hitler was supreme warlord and dictator of Germany, while at the same time being head of the army – and so in theory subordinate to Keitel. In practice Hitler and OKH came to have command of all forces in the war against the Soviet Union, while OKW dealt with everywhere else.

In fact, OKH was dependent on Hitler mostly for strategic direction, while the nitty-gritty of its tasks was in the hands of Kurt Zeitzler. Zeitzler was a master of the often tedious business of logistics. He could organize supplies to be moved across great distances with remarkable speed and knew how much petrol a panzer division would need to keep fighting. Zeitzler knew his business and how to achieve it, and when dealing with these sorts of technical matters was one of the few men who regularly stood up to Hitler. The two had some fiery disputes, after some of which Hitler backed down.

Under OKH the Eastern Front was in the hands of three large commands. Army Group North was commanded by Field Marshal Georg von Küchler. It comprised the 16th Army and 18th Army and was relatively inactive. The siege of Leningrad was its main concern. The siege had begun in September 1941 and was still dragging on in early 1943. Elsewhere along his line, von Küchler lacked the resources to do anything much other than dig in and hope the Soviets did not attack.

Army Group Centre was commanded by Günther von Kluge and was a substantially more powerful force, comprising 2nd Panzer Army, 3rd Panzer Army, 4th Army, 9th Army and LIX Army Corps. It held the line from Smolensk to Oryol and had been responsible for protecting the northern flank of the advance that ended at Stalingrad. Its units were well equipped, rested and up to full complement.

Army Group South was in the process of reorganizing in January 1943. It was commanded by Erich von Manstein, one of Germany's most talented senior generals. The units of Army Group South were exhausted after the fighting of 1942, short on equipment and lacking supplies. Its key 6th Army was bottled up in Stalingrad, and on 2 February it surrendered.

A fourth major unit, Army Group A, was in the Crimea and neighbouring areas of the Kuban to the south of Manstein's Army Group South. This smaller unit was commanded by Paul von Kleist. Manstein and Kleist bickered over the boundaries between their commands and who should have control of which units. Hitler came down on the side of Kleist because he wanted to keep a firm grip on the Crimea, which blocked a Soviet advance on key oilfields that were supplying the German war effort.

On 6 February Hitler summoned Manstein to OKH for a meeting. Manstein approached the meeting with some foreboding. His army group was in something of a mess and he had been taking chances, not all of which had paid off. Most concerning of all was the fact that Manstein had recently developed his own idiosyncratic way of dealing with OKH. Manstein had noticed that Hitler and OKH rarely flatly turned down a request. If a general suggested something with which Hitler did not agree, OKH simply refused to respond. This way, whether the general took the suggested action or not, he could be blamed if things went wrong. Manstein had adopted the ruse of ending each request with a sentence stating that unless he heard from OKH by a set date that they disagreed, he would assume that they were giving him permission to do whatever he suggested. In this way, Manstein had been able to retreat, counter-attack and reform his units as he wished.

Now Hitler wanted to see him and had sent an aircraft to carry him to the meeting. Other generals had answered a similar summons only to find themselves summarily sacked.

In fact Manstein found Hitler in calm and contemplative

mood. Drawing on reports from OKH staff, Hitler filled Manstein in on the logistical situation, particularly the production figures of new armoured vehicles, before moving on to discuss the military situation in Manstein's command area. Several different options were discussed. Manstein emphasized the weakness of his forces and the vast front that he was expected to hold. Eventually Hitler gave Manstein permission to withdraw men from some isolated positions, but insisted that the two cities of Kharkov and Kursk should be held. The meeting ended amicably, after which Manstein returned to his own headquarters.

Soviet movements

So long as the German 6th Army had held out in Stalingrad, the Soviets had kept the bulk of their forces around that unhappy city. Once the Germans surrendered, the Soviets were free to move their armies against the main front. The attack began at Voronezh, where the Soviets broke through a section of front held by the Hungarians and began pushing west toward the town of Kursk. Another assault began further south at Millerovo. Again the Soviets broke through the sparsely held front line and drove west between the Don and Donets toward the industrial city of Kharkov.

Driving onwards across weakly protected steppes, the Soviets next thrust forwards to produce a salient between Oryol and Kursk, a few days after a second thrust had outflanked Kursk to the south; not long afterwards, the city of Kursk duly fell to the Soviets.

The fall of Kursk formed a huge bulge in the line north of

Kharkov, which was quite clearly going to be the Soviets' next target. Kharkov was held by what on paper looked like a formidable force. Three elite SS panzer divisions – the Leibstandarte, Das Reich and Totenkopf – were positioned around the city under the command of General Hubert Lanz. However, the units were short on supplies, and communications with Manstein's headquarters had broken down.

Further Soviet advances were pushing into territory supposedly held by the Germans. A tank division reached Krasnoarmeiskoye, south of Kharkov, while large cavalry forces ranged widely across the lands south and east of Kharkov. On 15 February the SS panzers abandoned Kharkov.

Hitler's fury

Two days later Hitler and Zeitzler arrived by plane at Manstein's headquarters at Zaporozhye to discuss the situation. This time Manstein was sure that he was in for trouble since Kursk and Kharkov had both been lost. In fact it was Lanz who was fired, not Manstein. With that sacking out of the way, Hitler plunged into a detailed discussion of the crumbling situation. The retreat must stop, Hitler ordered, and it must stop at once.

Hitler had done his homework. He knew that the SS Panzer divisions had been receiving new tanks and crews, and the rate at which they had been arriving. He knew that Manstein had pulled the 4th Panzer Army out of the front line and that it had been enjoying two weeks of rest. He knew, too, that the 1st Panzer Army was standing on the defensive, with only one division actually engaged. Why, he demanded to know, were these forces not stopping the Soviet advance? Why was ground being lost, and industrial cities along with it? Did Manstein not understand the loss of prestige to the German army and the boost to Red Army morale that the Soviet advances caused?

Manstein was ready for the Führer's onslaught. He got out a map and explained the lie of the land, where the rivers ran and where supply railways were to be found. He pointed out that the Soviet advances so far had been mostly due west from the River Don. The roads and railways did not go in that direction, making the Soviet supply lines very difficult to organize. The Soviets simply could not bring up enough fuel, ammunition and food to continue going west. In any case, Manstein asked rhetorically, where were they going to go? There were only the vast Ukrainian wheatfields ahead of them.

Manstein then pointed south. The Soviets, he explained, must be planning to turn south. They would cross the River Dnieper, perhaps near Dnepropetrovsk, then head for the Black Sea coast. If they succeeded in getting there, they would have cut off almost all of Manstein's command, just as they had recently cut off the 6th Army at Stalingrad. That, Manstein said, was what the Soviets were planning to do. And Manstein was ready for them.

The reason he had been holding his panzers back was to keep them fresh for a daring strike. When the Soviets turned south, Manstein would unleash his panzers to cut them off from their base. Short on supplies and low on fuel, the Soviets would be surrounded and wiped out in days.

Then, Manstein pointed out, the spring thaw would come

and turn the roads into muddy quagmires that made all large-scale military movements impossible. Six weeks of inactivity would follow, during which time the reinforcements that Hitler had promised at the earlier meeting would arrive. When the dry weather came, the Germans would again be on a parity with the Soviets. The front would have been stabilized and all would be well.

At first Hitler did not accept Manstein's argument. Three days of intense debate took place. Eventually Hitler agreed with Manstein's plan. As Hitler walked out to his private aircraft to return to OKH he stopped and listened. He could hear gunfire to the north. The advancing Soviet cavalry scouts with horse artillery support were only 8 km (5 miles) away. It was the closest that Hitler got to the fighting during the entire war until the final Armaggedon in Berlin in 1945. After a final handshake with Manstein he was off.

Manstein's plan in action

With Hitler gone, Manstein got back to running his battle. After mounting a minor attack to let the Soviets know that it was at Taganrog on the Don, the 4th Panzer Army was moved rapidly by rail to Zaporozhye. The SS panzer divisions were similarly moved quickly to Poltava. This put the two armoured formations to north and south of the advancing Soviet columns. The Soviet advance had, meanwhile, turned south just as Manstein had predicted, with the lead cavalry patrols reaching Dnepropetrovsk.

On 21 February Manstein struck. The 4th Panzer Army went north, the SS panzers drove east and the two met a week later. Two entire Soviet armies were cut off. The Germans were short on infantry to seal the trap, so tens of thousands of Soviets were able to slip through the net. The Soviets had to leave behind their equipment, however, giving the Germans a gift of 615 tanks and 354 guns. Around 30,000 Soviet soldiers had been killed for trifling German losses.

Manstein now moved to exploit his victory. He turned his panzers to advance north along the west bank of the Donets and clear it of Soviets. On 13 March Kharkov was recaptured, and on 16 March Belgorod was taken. Then the spring thaw came, the roads turned to mud and Manstein's panzers squelched to a halt. Manstein had hoped to capture Kursk as well, but it was still in Soviet hands.

With the mud stopping all serious fighting for several weeks, the German High Command was free to spend some time planning what to do next.

Hitler was unusually quiet during these weeks. His stragetic plans for 1940, 1941 and 1942 had been brilliant in concept, but only the first had been translated into reality by his army commanders. He now seemed to be unable to come up with a new plan of strategic sweep that stood any real chance of winning the war.

Instead Hitler devoted his energies to overseeing the production of new weapons that were being developed in conditions of great secrecy. Some of these 'secret weapons', such as the Tiger and Panther tanks, were about to enter service. Others, including the V-1 and V-2 rockets , were in the early stages of development. A few, such as the programme to produce an atomic bomb, had run into such serious technical problems that they were on the verge of being abandoned. All of them attracted Hitler's personal attention at this time. Some benefited from Hitler's enthusiasm as resources were poured into their development, others – most notably the Me-262 jet fighter – suffered delays when Hitler demanded unfeasible modifications.

The business of planning what to do on the Eastern Front, meanwhile, fell to the professional military men.

Manstein was convinced that the Soviets would launch a summer offensive in his southern area. He developed what he termed a 'backhand' plan. Manstein wanted to withdraw his main forces west to the Dnieper, leaving only light forces in the vast eastern Ukraine in Kharkov and further south. When the Soviets attacked, Manstein planned to pull his light forces back, making a show of fighting a rearguard action with poorly equipped forces.

This, Manstein thought, would fool the Soviets into thinking that the German forces had not recovered properly from the losses of 1942. They would therefore push their main force into the developing bulge in the line on the north coast of the Black Sea, ready to launch a devastating drive north to roll up the entire Eastern Front. Once the Soviets were in position, Manstein would finally let loose his own panzers to cut off the bulge, surround the Soviets and destroy the bulk of their entire army. It would be like the heady days of summer 1941 all over again.

Zeitzler, with his eye as ever on supply and logistical issues, thought it much more likely that the Soviets would attack further north, perhaps near Oryol or KCrsk. Soviet supply

German infantry advance during the Battle of Kursk supported by a StuG III. The StuG III was a powerful 75mm cannon mounted on the chassis of the Panzer III and was able to provide mobile, close support fire for the infantry.

lines were better there than in the south. Such an offensive would mean that Manstein's panzers would be in the wrong place to cut them off. A more conventional battle would result, with no real advantage to the Germans. He told Manstein to think again.

Erich von Manstein (1887–1973)

Manstein is generally recognized to have been the finest strategist of the war. He was born into an ancient family of Prussian aristocracy, which left him little choice of career. In the First World War, Manstein was wounded while fighting the Russians and thereafter served on the staff. He served with infantry and cavalry, ending the war as Chief of Staff to an infantry division. After the war he went home, proposed to a young woman three days after meeting her (their marriage lasted happily to her death in 1966) and played a key role in restructuring the army.

When the Nazis began a massive growth in the army, Manstein was on the general staff and again played a key role in restructuring the German army. It was Manstein who developed the strategic complement to Guderian's panzer tactics by arguing that the panzer units needed to be concentrated together to launch a devastating offensive on a narrow frontage at a key point. The result of this idea being put into practice was the collapse of Poland in 1939 and of France in 1940.

For the invasion of Russia, Manstein was given command of a panzer corps. It has been argued that his absence from the general staff during the crucial months of planning meant that the German offensive made key strategic mistakes which led to the failure to defeat the Soviets in a single campaign. It was not until the spring of 1943 that Manstein's strategic flair was seen again in the brilliantly executed counter-attack after the fall of Stalingrad.

Erich von Manstein, commander of Army Group South during the Battle of Kursk.

After Kursk, Manstein retained command of Army Group South, but he increasingly came to see that the war was lost and had long and bitter arguments with Hitler. Finally, Hitler fired Manstein in March 1944. At the Nuremburg Trials, Manstein spoke skilfully and forcefully to make the point that the Germany army had been kept largely in ignorance of the atrocities and genocide being carried out by the Nazi Party in conquered territories. The extent to which German soldiers and officers in particular knew about the Holocaust and other atrocities has been a bone of contention ever since.

Convicted of war crimes, Manstein was released in 1950 and wrote *Lost Victories*, a highly acclaimed military history of the war from the German point of view. He then for a third time played a key role in restructuring the German army before finally retiring in 1958.

Manstein's next plan was to continue where he had left off when the spring thaw had arrived. As soon as the dry weather made movements possible he would launch a small, quick strike north up the Donets to capture Kursk and clear the west bank of enemy forces. That would have the advantage of upsetting whatever offensive plans the Soviets might have for later in the summer and mean that any enemy advance would have to start with the uneviable task of crossing a major river under fire.

Hitler's opinion, when he was asked, was in favour of the new plan. He worried that a Soviet advance along the north shore of the Black Sea, even one that was merely temporary, might cause political problems with Romania and Turkey. He was not, however, apparently very keen on the idea.

Zeitzler now turned to Kluge of Army Group Centre. His area of command included Oryol, north of Kursk. Any attack by Manstein from the south would be helped enormously if Kluge launched a diversionary attack from the north to draw off Soviet forces. Kluge was as half-heartedly supportive as Hitler. He pointed out that his forces were under strength and that the salient he held around Oryol was a tempting target for a Soviet offensive. And what, he wanted to know, about all those marvellous secret weapons – the Tiger and the Panther – that he had been promised he would get in spring 1943? Spring was almost here, so where were they?

Chapter 2

PANZER FORCE

The fighting of 1942 had revealed some serious deficiencies in Germany's much-admired panzers. The use of the panzers on the battlefield in the standard *blitzkrieg* tactics was as effective as ever, but losses among the tanks had been rising steadily. This was partly a result of the arrival of the Soviet T-34 medium tank, but was also due to the increasing numbers of anti-tank guns that the Soviets were deploying in lavish numbers.

The panzers being used by the Germans were all fairly old. The Panzer II had been designed in 1934, the Panzer III in 1935 and the Panzer IV in 1936. Together they made for a compact and effective fighting team.

The Panzer II was designed to scout ahead of the main force and to take on enemy infantry and artillery. It had 30 mm steel armour that provided protection against machine-guns and most artillery, though not against specialist anti-tank guns. It mounted a 20 mm cannon and a 7.92 mm machine-gun. Neither was effective against enemy tanks or bunkers, but the cannon could bring down buildings and destroy thin-skinned vehicles. It had a road weight of 8 tonnes.

The real value of the Panzer II was its mobility. It could travel 200 km (125 miles) without refuelling and on roads could reach 50 km/h (30 mph), both impressive figures for contemporary tanks. The Panzer II was therefore ideal for racing ahead of the main panzer punch to spread confusion and destruction in the rear areas of the enemy forces. It would destroy enemy communications, supply lines and command centres, pulling back as soon as it encountered enemy armour or anti-tank weaponry. During the invasion of France many units of Panzer II were erroneously identified by the French as being Panzer III or even Panzer IV. The French soldiers, thinking they were up against a more formidable tank than they were, fled.

The Panzer III was designed to be a tank-killer, destroying the enemy armoured vehicles in battle, as well as tackling anti-tank guns. The 50 mm gun was equipped to fire both armour-piercing and high-explosive shells. The tank also had two 7.92 mm machine-guns to take on infantry or thin-skinned vehicles.

The armour was mostly 50 mm (2 inches) thick, but up to 70 mm (2¾ inches) in vulnerable areas. This made the tank proof against almost all anti-tank weapons when it entered service in 1937, but by 1942 newer weapons made it vulnerable – especially from the rear. Its weight was around 20 tonnes, depending on the model, and it could reach 39 km/h (24 mph) on roads.

The Panzer IV was intended to be the main battle tank of the German army. While the Panzer II scouted ahead and the Panzer III swatted aside anti-tank weaponry, the Panzer IV was to smash enemy strongpoints, blast bunkers and destroy everything in its path. To achieve this it had a 75 mm cannon and two 7.92 mm machine-guns.

The 25-tonne tank had 80-mm (3¼-inch) armour on its front and 30-mm (1¼-inch) armour on the flanks. This made it impervious to most weaponry head-on, but it was more vulnerable when attacked from the flank or rear.

A battalion of Tiger I tanks arrives by rail in July 1943 to take part in the Battle of Kursk. Note the wider tracks that were fitted to tanks destined to fight on the rough and often boggy terrain of the Eastern Front.

One feature not immediately obvious from the outside was of crucial importance: all these tanks had roomy turrets, so that there was space for a commander who did not have to double up as gunner or loader, as he did in tanks of other nations. There was also space for a two-way radio set. This meant that each tank had a commander who could devote his time fully to keeping an eye on what was going on and deciding what to do about it. By keeping in two-way touch with other tanks and his unit commander, the tank captain could warn others of peril or call in support when needed. This feature alone accounted for much of the success of the panzers in battle.

The combination of these three types had been developed in the 1930s by the talented German tank officer Heinz Guderian, who had overseen both the development of the tanks and the devising of tactics to use them in action.

Unleashing the Tiger

Successful as the trio of panzers had been, improvements were now needed. The lavish proliferation of Soviet anti-tank guns meant that the Germans needed a new, more heavily armoured tank that could punch a hole in the enemy defences by trundling up to the anti-tank guns and blasting them out of existence without itself being vulnerable to their fire.

The specification for this new monster called for 120-mm (4¾-inch) armour on the front and turret, with lesser but still effective armour elsewhere. To tackle enemy tanks and strong-points the new tank was to have an 88 mm cannon. To ensure that this heavy tank did not bog down on the soft ground of the Eastern Front, it was given special wide tracks.

The resulting vehicle was dubbed the Tiger, though its official designation was Panzer VI. It was to become perhaps the most awesome tank of the war and would soon acquire a reputation for being almost invulnerable in open combat as well as being able to dish out terrific firepower.

In combat, the Tiger was to be deployed in relatively small numbers. The Tigers would form the apex of a triangular formation, in which other tank designs formed the wider base and filled the centre. The Tigers would punch a hole through enemy anti-tank defences, then turn aside to open up and keep open a gap through which the other tanks could advance to fan out and destroy enemy formations.

The other new panzer entering service early in 1943 was the Panther, the Panzer V. The Panther was designed to replace the Panzer IV as the main battle tank, able to tackle enemy infantry and strongpoints but also to take on the roles of the Panzer III and Panzer II in fighting enemy tanks and racing ahead to exploit a breakthrough.

This 44-tonne tank had sloped armour equivalent to 140 mm (5½ inches) of steel on its front and was armed with a 75 mm cannon, plus two machine-guns. It could reach more than 50 km/h (30 mph) on roads and travel 250 km (155 miles) without refuelling. The Panther is generally reckoned to have been the best tank of the war, combining speed and manoeuvrability with hitting power.

As a replacement for the Panzer II, the Germans planned the Leopard. This was to be a cut-down, 21-tonne version of the Panther design equipped with a 50 mm gun. A lot of time and effort went into this project, but in the end it was not put into production. It was decided that scouting could be carried out by armoured cars instead.

The abortive Leopard project was but one factor that delayed the appearance of the new generation of panzers on the battlefield. Until Albert Speer got a grip on things as minister of armaments in the summer of 1942, German war industry was a mess of competing firms and back-stabbing officials as eager to boost their own career prospects as to run down those of others.

The end result was that production of the Panther was delayed by almost a year, while the Tiger was never produced in the numbers envisaged. Even worse, the Panther was running so late that there was no time to put it through the usual field trials before it entered production. Many early examples suffered almost continual breakdown and teething problems when they did enter service just in time for Kursk.

A further problem affecting panzer production came out of the success of a stopgap hybrid vehicle that had first seen action in 1942. This was the Marder III. Up until 1942 the Germans had been using several hundred captured Czech LT38 tanks in the same role as the Panzer II. However, the 37 mm cannon of the LT38 was quickly recognized to be obsolete. At the same time the German artillerymen were finding that their conventional 75 mm anti-tank gun, which was towed into action behind a truck carrying crew and ammunition, was hopeless on the poor roads and boggy ground of Russia.

Self-propelled guns

In what was at the time seen as a temporary, stopgap measure, the artillerymen mounted some 75 mm guns on top of the chassis of the LT38 to produce the Marder III. The result was a tracked vehicle that could cope with the poor surface conditions in Russia but could also carry the anti-tank gun. The weapon proved to be effective when accompanying infantry into action, as it could both knock out enemy tanks and tackle strongpoints with high explosive.

German designers rapidly developed the concept to produce two new weapons. The first was the Sturmgeschütz, or assault gun. This saw a 75 mm artillery gun mounted on a tank chassis. It was designed to accompany infantry into action, blasting apart enemy bunkers or strong points. The other concept was the Jagdpanzer, or tank-hunter – which was similar but mounted an anti-tank gun.

Both vehicles had their gun mounted in an armoured casement that allowed it to fire forwards only, the gun being aimed by altering the position of the entire vehicle. Lacking all the complicated machinery and armour of a turret, the Sturmgeschütz and Jagdpanzer were much cheaper and quicker to manufacture than a tank. This made them attractive to the army as a quick and cost-effective way to increase the firepower of units. By the start of 1943 one-third of tanks in all panzer units had been replaced by Jagdpanzers, while the artillery were quickly ditching their towed guns in favour of Sturmgeschützes.

A key weakness of these weapons was that they could not traverse their main weaponry quickly. Even worse was the lack of a machine-gun, which left them vulnerable to enemy infantry armed with close-range anti-tank weapons.

The concept of the self-propelled gun, as these weapons are collectively known to English-speaking military, came to dominate theories of assault tactics in the German army. With the encouragement of artillery staff keen to retain their prestige and budgets, the infantry came to consider that Sturmgeschützes would be essential to any future assault. Experience of Soviet strong points showed that they could be very strong indeed, which led to the development of the Ferdinand, better known by its nickname of 'Elefant'.

It was not just the artillery staff who were playing politics with weapon design. Dr Ferdinand Porsche – the highly talented car designer – had decided to have a go at designing armoured vehicles. His big project for 1942 had been a design for the Tiger, but it had been rejected by the army as being too complex to be properly maintained under battlefield conditions.

Porsche then went to see Hitler – who greatly admired his car designs – and so managed to get permission to undertake a couple of new projects by way of compensation for his rejected Tiger. The first of these was a super-heavy panzer designed to act as a mobile strongpoint weighing just over 160 tonnes. That project did not get beyond the prototype stage, but the second did. This was the Ferdinand.

In concept the Ferdinand was relatively simple. It consisted of the chassis for the reject Porsche Tiger, on top of which was mounted one of Krupp's famous 88 mm cannons. These guns could fire armour-piercing, high-explosive or anti-aircraft shells with equal success and have been consistently rated among the best heavy guns ever produced. In line with the Sturmgeschütz concept, the gun was mounted in a fixed mounting that gave it a limited traverse. The vehicle also lacked a machine-gun, though the theorists declared that this would not be a problem because the vehicle would be accompanied into battle by supporting mechanized infantry, the panzergrenadiers.

In fact the Elefant would prove to be one of the most disastrous combat vehicles to go into action. It had a further deleterious effect on the German military, since the squabbling that had accompanied its production and the manufacturing resources it consumed held back production of the far more effective Panther.

Another problem with the increasing reliance on Jagdpanzers in panzer units was that the production and design of these weapons remained under the control of the artillery, while their use was the province of the panzer men. Inevitably the artillery staff officers controlling supply and repair gave priority to the artillery units, meaning that the panzer units were often chronically short of Jagdpanzers.

Guderian: fall and rise

Hitler had appointed Speer to control production. Now he decided he needed a military man to get a grip on design, allocation and use of the new tanks. He chose Heinz Guderian, who had overseen the design and production of the earlier generation of panzers.

Although Guderian was widely recognized as among the best tank commanders of the war, his career had not been entirely smooth. After great success in the opening stages of the war in Russia, he fell from favour during the battle for Moscow. On 26 December 1941 he was relieved of his command of Panzergruppe 2. The circumstances are still not entirely clear, but Guderian ever after harboured a grudge against his immediate superior, Kluge. Guderian had been effectively unemployed ever since.

Two days after he saw Manstein at Zaporozhye, Hitler interviewed Guderian at OKH. Hitler began with, for him, an almost unprecedented apology for the 'misunderstandings' that had resulted in Guderian being left without work for so long. He then went on to tell the astonished Guderian that he had been re-reading his works on tank warfare and become convinced that Guderian was close to being a genius. 'I need you,' declared Hitler.

Hitler then offered Guderian the job – which until this point had not existed – of Inspector General of Armoured Troops. Guderian's task was awesome, but so were the powers given to him. He was to be responsible for tank design and production, the training of crews, tactical deployments and anything else that touched on the effectiveness in battle of the panzer units.

To allow him to carry out this difficult task, Guderian was given the rank of an army commander and the even rarer right to see the Führer whenever he wished.

The entire interview lasted just 45 minutes before Guderian was ushered out and shown the newly decorated offices that had been prepared for him and the staff that he was free to choose. Guderian at once set to work. It was not until some days later that he realized that somebody at OKH, he never found out who, had doctored his orders after they were dictated by Hitler to exclude from his remit the assault guns and tank-hunter guns that remained under the control of the artillery branch of the army. It was a move that was to have disastrous results at Kursk.

Nevertheless, Guderian's work soon bore fruit. He insisted that all panzer units be periodically taken out of the front line and given leave in rest areas. He also organized for the panzers themselves to be pulled out for major overhauls and upgrades. Working with Speer, Guderian reduced the number of different variants of the generation of panzers and so speeded up production.

Plans for Kursk offensive

Morale, numbers and ability soared. The panzer force was rapidly returning to its effectiveness of old. But still Guderian was not satisfied. After studying intelligence reports to which his new position entitled him, he came to the conclusion that the German army, or at least its crucial panzer arm, could not mount an operation that stood a realistic chance of crushing the Soviets within the next 12 months. In March 1943 he circulated a note to Hitler and a small number of senior officers that concluded: 'The task for 1943 is to build up a large number of panzer divisions with complete combat efficiency, capable of making attacks with limited objectives. For 1944 we must prepare to launch large-scale attacks to win the war.'

Keitel, from OKW, agreed. He knew that the Allies in the Mediterranean were likely to invade either Greece or Italy in the near future and was worried about the possibility of Allied landings in France as well. He did not want to see reserves thrown at the Eastern Front.

On the other hand, Zeitzler and several other senior staff officers at OKH were aghast. The idea that the magnificent German army was not fit to mount a major operation at all in 1943 was, they thought, tantamount to treason. They quickly found ways to pick holes in Guderian's report. The personal animosity with Kluge played a role, as he cheerfully denounced his rival's ideas and at the same time sought to gain the Führer's favour by promising great things for the summer of 1943.

Guderian had inadvertently goaded the German High Command into doing exactly what he thought they should not do: launch a major offensive in 1943.

Thus it was that during the non-combat weeks of the spring thaw, Zeitzler at OKH began looking around for a plan for a major offensive to prove Guderian and Keitel wrong and, as he saw it, rescue the prestige of the German army. Zeitzler had a willing ally in Kluge, who not only detested Guderian but was anxious to get his Army Group Centre into action after it had stood largely idle throughout 1942.

Together Zeitzler and Kluge dusted off Manstein's plans for an assault on Kursk. They recognized that the chance of a swift, surprise strike had gone since the spring thaw was now over and dry weather had come. Instead they worked the concept up into a fairly major offensive aimed at eliminating the entire Kursk salient by an attack launched by Kluge in the north and Manstein in the south. The offensive was designed both to clear the west bank of the Donets and to inflict such losses on the Soviets that they could not themselves mount a major offensive that year.

This new concept, codename Operation *Zitadelle*, was presented to a staff conference in the first week of April. Much to the annoyance of Zeitzler and Kluge, Manstein spoke against it and revived his idea of a 'backhand' campaign in the south. Kluge at once began a whispering campaign against Manstein, saying that he favoured the 'backhand' plan only as it would give all the glory to his own army group.

On 11 April, Zeitzler submitted to Hitler a memo formally suggesting Operation *Zitadelle*. The attack would be launched in May by the 9th Army from Army Group Centre in the north and the 4th Panzer Army from Army Group South to the south. A total of ten panzer divisions would be involved. Hitler responded by asking questions – a tactic he often used to delay making a decision on a matter he did not like.

While Zeitzler set about responding to Hitler's queries and concerns, Hitler sent his personal adjutant, Rudolf Schmundt, off on a series of visits to army commanders on the Eastern Front. Officially the purpose of the tour was to raise morale and assure commanders of Hitler's personal concern for them and the men under their command. In fact Schmundt's main purpose was to sound out opinion on *Zitadelle*.

Every army commander that Schmundt spoke to was in favour of *Zitadelle*, with two exceptions. Manstein repeated his view that a surprise attack in April would have been useful and successful, but that the gains were now outweighed by the risks.

Rather more surprising was the opposition of Walter Model, commander of the 9th Army – which would form the northern prong of the attack. Far from relishing the opportunity to get into action and gain glory by defeating the Red Army, Model was deeply pessimistic about the chances of success. He had gone to the front line himself to view the enemy defences and had spent many hours studying aerial photos. The Soviet defensive works were, Model declared, invulnerable. An attack would be a useless waste of lives.

Hitler used these concerns to raise new questions and concerns with Zeitzler. The OKH staff came back with the assertion that the new generation of panzers could smash the Soviet defences wide open; Model did not understand their power in battle. They also used the new argument that since the Soviets were building strong defences, the target must be worth attacking.

Still Hitler was unconvinced. Zeitzler arranged for a strategy conference to be held in Munich on 3 May. The topic for discussion was ostensibly overall war strategy for 1943. In reality the aim was to persuade Hitler to go ahead with *Zitadelle*. Present were Zeitzler, Kluge, Manstein and Guderian as well as a host of senior staff officers. Zeitzler had arranged the timing to ensure that Model could not attend and had handpicked the staff officers that supported his plans.

Hitler listened to the enthusiastic urgings of the majority, to Manstein's misgivings and Guderian's opposition. Then he seized on one point that Kluge had made. If the new generation of panzers could break open even the toughest Soviet defences, how was production of the new tanks coming along? All eyes turned to Speer.

Speer reported that the Tigers were being produced according to plan, but that there had been difficulties with the Panther. Only 100 of them had been delivered to the army. However, he went on, the problems had now been solved and he could now say definitely that 320 Panthers would be delivered by the end of May and that production would then continue at between 150 and 200 each month. A quick comparison with Kluge's figures showed that enough Panthers would have been delivered by the middle of June.

Hitler told Zeitzler to proceed with preparations for *Zitadelle*, but that a final decision on whether or not to go ahead would be made in early June and would be dependent on the Panthers arriving on time.

A week later Guderian was again at a conference with Hitler, this time updating the Führer on more mundane matters of panzer design and crew training. As the conference broke up, Guderian took the opportunity to speak privately to Hitler. According to Guderian's later memoirs, he asked Hitler why he was intending to attack anywhere in 1943.

'We have to launch an attack of some sort for political reasons,' replied Hitler.

'But why Kursk?' demanded Guderian. 'How many people do you think even know where Kursk is? It is a matter of profound indifference to the world whether we hold Kursk or not. I repeat my question. Why do we want to attack in the East at all this year?'

'You're quite right,' replied Hitler. 'Whenever I think of this attack my stomach turns over.'

'In that case your reaction to the problem is the correct one. Leave it alone!' concluded Guderian.

Hitler nodded slowly. 'I have by no means committed myself,' he said.

Unstoppable momentum

But the *Zitadelle* project had acquired a momentum of its own. As Zeitzler and his team at OKH embarked on the detailed planning of which division would attack where and how they would get their supplies, the bureaucracy of the German army became enthused by the project. The view spread among senior officers that the offensive was certain to be a success. As the enthusiasm spread, so did the assumption that approval for the assault had already been given.

Heinz Guderian (1888–1954)

Born the son of a career army officer, Guderian joined his father's unit in 1907. When war came in 1914 he was serving in a cavalry unit, and soon transferred to the staff. A series of disagreements with his superiors became bitter when he was proved correct, so his superiors shunted him off into a junior position in military intelligence. After the war he returned to staff work and during the 1920s and 1930s became obsessed with the potential of motorized warfare. His epochal book *Achtung – Panzer*, published in 1937, laid out the fundamentals of *blitzkrieg* tactics.

For the invasion of Poland in 1939, Guderian was given a corps comprising one panzer and two motorized infantry divisions. His rapid advances, sweeping manoeuvres and swift victories won him the nickname 'Hurrying Heinz' and the command of the panzer spearhead in the invasion of France in 1940. The swift collapse of France was largely due to Guderian's handling of the panzers. For the invasion of the Soviet Union, Guderian advocated a series of massive armoured punches to drive fast and far into Russia, but was overruled and ordered instead to destroy the Soviet army on the frontiers. He objected, his arguments becoming fiercer and more inflexible as the planning progressed. In the event he was proved to have been correct, though this did not become clear until some months into the campaign. As in 1915, he was eventually sacked for having been right. It was not until after the disaster of Stalingrad that Hitler intervened to overrule the generals and recall Guderian.

After Kursk, Guderian remained in charge of armoured troops until in July 1944 he was promoted to be Chief of Staff of the German army. In that position he continued to argue with Hitler, and was increasingly ignored. He was fired again on 28 March 1945, by which time the war was effectively over. He did not face war crimes charges after the war and spent his retirement speaking to events of retired soldiers in both Germany and Britain.

Heinz Guderian pictured in a transport aircraft as he undertakes a tour of inspection of panzer troops near Kharkov in April 1943.

This bureaucratic momentum reached such a pitch that the operation became virtually certain, no matter that even Hitler thought he had not given final permission. On 10 June aerial reconnaissance photos showed that the Soviet defences around Kursk were more formidable than had been previously thought by anyone except Molder. The new evidence persuaded Manstein. He now moved from being sceptical to being downright hostile to the plan. He told Zeitzler and Hitler that the offensive was doomed to failure and must not go ahead.

But it was too late. Instead of cancelling the *Zitadelle* attack, OKH merely postponed it to allow time for two more full battalions of Panther tanks to arrive at the front. It did not seem to occur to anyone in the German High Command that if they delayed to allow themselves more time to prepare, then it would also give the Soviets more time to prepare.

And preparing is what the Soviets were doing.

Chapter 3

A WAITING GAME

Just as the Germans were debating, disagreeing and hesitating over their plans for the summer of 1943, so were the Soviets. They had just achieved the seemingly impossible by completing the entire annihilation of the crack German 6th Army at Stalingrad, and had followed that up by a rapid advance to take Kursk and Kharkov. The subsequent crushing of their forward units by Manstein on the approaches to the Dnieper had somewhat curbed Soviet ambitions, but done little to dent their growing confidence and rising morale.

War of attrition

The system of high command in the Red Army was considerably more straightforward than in the German and much less prone to outside interference. The supreme command body was the *Stavka Verkhovnovo Komandovaniya* (Supreme Command of the Armed Forces), which is generally referred to as the Stavka. This was a committee chaired by Defence Minister Timoshenko and on which sat the head of the army, head of the navy and head of the air force along with a selection of military marshals.

Joseph Stalin, dictator of the Soviet Union, was a member of the Stavka but did not always attend and rarely took much part in proceedings other than to ask questions. Stalin's role was, therefore, very different from that of Hitler who took a lead role in strategic decisions and meddled constantly in other matters from supply to weapons design to tactical deployments.

Stalin had early on decided that the war would be won not so much on the battlefield as on the factory floor. He wanted the war to be one of grinding attrition, relying on the vast resources of the Soviet Union to produce more weapons and men than Germany could. Stalin shifted talented men and vast resources into the business of producing weapons – all other forms of production or agriculture were starved of both. As cold-blooded decisions went, this was entirely sensible though it inevitably condemned Stalin's people to massive losses of men, equipment and wealth.

The losses were made worse by the Stavka's acceptance that Soviet equipment was generally inferior to that of the Germans and that they would spend less time training their men. An acceptance grew that losses were immaterial, so long as casualties were inflicted on the enemy.

By the time of the spring thaw in 1943, the Soviets had built up numerically awesome strength. They had more than 6 million men in the field, supported by 15,000 tanks, 33,000 field guns and 3,500 aircraft. The Germans had only 2.6 million men, 2,200 tanks and 6,400 guns plus 2,200 aircraft.

Intelligence – Bletchley Park and beyond

In deciding what to do with this strength come the spring of 1943, the Soviets had critical advantages over the Germans in terms of intelligence. While the Germans relied on aerial photography to find out what the Soviets were up to, the Soviets had a highly effective intelligence system.

Officially the prime source of information about German movements and intentions came by way of the British 'Ultra' system. The German armed forces used a complicated electro-mechanical rotor device to encrypt signals before they were transmitted by radio. They knew the signals were likely to be intercepted, but believed that the encryption was so sophisticated that the enemy would not be able to read the messages.

Essentially the Germans were correct, but careless handling by some German encoders and lapses in procedure allowed the British to crack some of the code. The British decrypters working at Bletchley Park in the English county of Buckinghamshire were never able to read all the signals and long periods occurred when they could read none at all, but as the war progressed they managed to decode more and more signals.

The nature of these signals limited what the British could learn. They could read radio signals sent from one German unit to another, between headquarters and subsidiary command posts or even from the Führer's personal office to OKH, but they had no real way of knowing the motives behind the signals. Troop movements and the build-up of supply dumps could be detected and monitored. These might mean that an offensive was imminent, or might mean that the Germans feared a Soviet attack.

Nevertheless the intercepted signals – codenamed Ultra – were so precious that the British government placed a severe and effective block on knowledge that the German codes had been broken. Many of the people working on decrypting or translating the signals were not told what they were doing. Each person was given one small part of the task to complete so that only a very few people had a complete overview of what was going on.

Once the messages had been translated and analysed, a report was written on what it was thought the messages meant. This report went to very few people. Even a person as exalted as Sir Arthur Harris, Commander of RAF Bomber Command, was not allowed to see the reports and had no idea that German messages were being intercepted. All he knew was that he had been given an order to attack a particular target at a particular time. Harris came to resent what he thought was political interference in how he was fighting the bomber campaign, and never understood what was really going on. Other senior commanders were in a similar situation.

The Soviets were passed information by the British that came from the Ultra system. They, too, were not told where the information came from and were kept entirely in the dark as to how the British got their intelligence. In the early stages of the war, the Soviets did not trust the intelligence given them by the British – especially as it was often incomplete.

In 1942, however, a British communist who was working for the Soviet GRU spy system was transferred from his post at the Foreign Office to Bletchley Park. John Cairncross now had access to the signals passing between OKW, OKH and Army Group headquarters. His task was to help in the analysis of these signals and the compilation of reports based on them. In fact he passed all the transcripts he saw straight to the GRU.

Useful as Ultra and Cairncross were to the Soviets, they were not their only source of information. The Lucy spy ring – so named as it was based in Lucerne in Switzerland – was also operating at this time. An enormous amount of mystery surrounds Lucy, and even today the truth behind what was going on is unclear. Given that the men and women involved were up against the Gestapo it is little wonder that they were so secretive.

The central figure was a German named Rudolf Roessler who had moved to live in Lucerne in 1933. Roessler made a living publishing pamphlets and books hostile to the Nazi regime. It was for this reason, Roessler later claimed, that he was approached in 1939 by two German army officers. The officers gave Roessler an 'Enigma' code machine and told him that they would be sending him top-secret signals from German military headquarters. They planned to designate Roessler as a fictitious military unit to explain the signals traffic. The officers then left and soon afterwards Roessler began receiving messages from them relating to high-level German troop movements.

Not entirely certain what to do with these messages, Roessler took them to an acquaintance who worked for the Swiss government. He put Roessler in touch with the Swiss intelligence services, which passed the material on to the British. In 1940 Roessler was approached by a man calling himself Taylor who said he was from Soviet intelligence. Taylor asked Roessler to give him copies of the signals as they came in, which Roessler then did.

In the summer of 1943 the Gestapo learned something of

The enigmatic Rudolf Roessler, who ran the Lucy spy ring out of Switzerland. The Lucy ring provided the Soviets with advance warning of the German attack at Kursk and enabled them to organize devastating defences. Roessler is shown here after his arrest by Swiss authorities in October 1943.

what was going on by intercepting radio signals being sent from Switzerland to Moscow. After some weeks of investigations and of applying pressure to the Swiss government, the Germans arranged for Roessler to be arrested and his premises searched. The Lucy spy ring collapsed.

Intelligence experts have never really been able to make much sense of the Lucy ring. The story offered by Roessler about the two mysterious German officers is so ridiculous that many simply don't believe it. Presumably, Roessler concocted the story to cover up how he really was getting his information. But wherever the Lucy information originated, it was genuine and of very high quality.

'Wear down the enemy'

As the Stavka considered its plans for the spring and summer of 1943, therefore, it had a very good idea of what the Germans were thinking and planning. It knew, for instance, about Manstein's original plan to assault Kursk when the thaw ended and so constructed defences to the south of the city. It knew also of his subsequent idea for a 'backhand' strategy in the south – which directly led them to cancel their own offensive that they had, indeed, been contemplating.

On 12 April a major conference was held at the Stavka at which the head of the Army General Staff, Georgi Zhukov, presented a report. After many hours of discussion between the senior army commanders, with Stalin playing his usual role at these events of listening intently, a decision was made.

Zhukov had deduced that the Germans would be forced to rely heavily on their panzers and aircraft in 1943. These arms had been built up steadily – largely due to Guderian – while the infantry had not yet recovered fully from Stalingrad. He therefore expected a large-scale assault by panzer forces that would have only limited objectives. Zhukov therefore dismissed entirely the idea of an early offensive by the Red Army.

'It would be better,' the report ran, 'if we were to wear down the enemy on our defence, destroy his tanks and then throw in fresh reserves to go over to a general offensive and decisively defeat the basic concentration of the enemy forces.' A long discussion then followed. In the early stages Stalin asked questions that Zhukov thought showed that he in fact favoured an early Soviet offensive, but he later fell silent and simply listened. In the end nearly everyone around the table came to agree with Zhukov, and Stalin nodded his approval.

Orders went out from the Stavka to all Red Army commanders that they were to dig in and prepare to face a panzer attack. The question remained, however, where would the blow fall?

Over the following weeks the Soviets received a steady stream of intelligence that showed the German High Command to be very interested in the area around Kursk. Although there was no clue as to exactly what the Germans were planning, the fact that they were building up detailed maps of the area, taking large numbers of aerial photos and assessing the strength of the Red Army around the city on an almost daily basis all pointed to the fact that Zeitzler at OKH was planning an operation there.

Zhukov and his team sat down to try to think themselves into German minds. Knowing what they did about German strength, German dispositions and German tactics, what was the most likely plan for the Germans to draw up? By the end of April they had come up with what they thought was going to be the German plan of attack. They changed their minds over detail as more intelligence came in, but the basic premise of the Soviet plan did not alter. And as events were to show, it was fairly close to what the German plan actually was.

The Soviets guessed that the German attack would come in two parts. To the north there would be an assault going south from near Glasunovka that would go by way of Ponyri to Kursk. A southern assault would start near Butovo, then drive north past Oboyan to meet the northern assault at Kursk. If these drives were successful, the converging panzer columns would cut off the huge Soviet forces positioned west of Kursk to defend the salient.

Evacuating the salient would mean that no Soviet forces would be vulnerable to being surrounded, but it would mean the Germans would not attack and so could not be ground down as Zhukov intended. Instead the Soviets kept large forces in the salient, but withdrew to the east their valuable tanks and guns, leaving behind infantry and cavalry. At the same time intensive efforts went into constructing defences in the areas where the German attacks were expected. The armoured forces withdrawn from the salient, together with new rein-forcements brought into the area from elsewhere, were formed into a mobile reserve placed some 80 km (50 miles) to the east, near Livny. From there it could be moved forwards to plug any gaps that occurred.

With the basic outlines of their plan in place, the Soviets then had to play a waiting game. At first Zhukov thought that the Germans would attack in late May, then perhaps in early June. Both dates came and went with no sign of the enemy.

Georgy Zhukov (1896–1974)

Zhukov was born into a peasant family. In 1915 he was conscripted into the Imperial Russian Army, where he was decorated for bravery. He joined the Red Army during the Russian Civil War and by its end was in command of a cavalry regiment. In the years of peace he saw steady if unspectacular promotion and by 1937 commanded a cavalry corps. In August 1939 he commanded the Soviets in the Battle of Khalkhin Gol, a large-scale border battle with the Japanese in the Far East. His victory there saw him promoted to be a senior general.

In 1941 Zhukov drew up a plan for an invasion of Germany and submitted it to the Stavka. It was still under consideration when Germany invaded the Soviet Union instead. Zhukov commanded the defence of Leningrad for some months, then oversaw the winter offensive that drove the Germans away from Moscow. Stalin then moved him to defend Stalingrad, and it was Zhukov who drew up the plans that led to the destruction of the German 6th Army in that city. Those successes led to Zhukov being made Deputy Commander-in-Chief of the Red Army. Thereafter he oversaw most of the key offensives of the Red Army. He was present when the Germans surrendered in Berlin on 8 May 1945.

After the war, Zhukov commanded the occupying Soviet troops in Germany until he suffered a heart attack in 1948. He had recovered by 1953 and was promoted to Deputy Defence Minister. At a meeting of the Politburo on 26 June 1953, shortly after Stalin's death, Nikita Khrushchev denounced the head of the secret police, Lavrenti Beria. It was Zhukov who

Georgi Zhukov, photographed in July 1943 while the Battle of Kursk was raging.

pulled out his gun and hustled Beria out of the room for a secret trial and execution. Zhukov later oversaw the Soviet invasion of Hungary in 1956. He then retired and spent his time hunting and fishing, though he sometimes took part in military parades and other events.

Stalin began to fret that they might have misinterpreted German intentions; perhaps the Germans were going to spend a quiet year rebuilding their forces ready for a massive offensive in 1944 – which was just what Guderian was advocating. If that were the case, the Soviets' best course of action was to launch their own offensives to inflict damage on the Germans and deny them the rest they craved. Zhukov disagreed. The Germans were going to attack, and they were going to attack Kursk.

It was just a matter of time.

Chapter 4

DIGGING FOR VICTORY

In preparing to meet the German offensive at Kursk, the Soviets put enormous efforts into constructing a deep network of defensive structures and forces. They were determined that they would learn the lessons of their defeats in 1941 and 1942.

In previous encounters with the German army, the Red Army had been comprehensively smashed in the early stages. German attacks had always succeeded; it was only later that the Soviets had been able to re-establish their lines. By retreating hundreds of kilometres, the Soviets stretched the German supply lines to their limit, exhausted the infantry and wore out the tanks. When the German advance was already grinding to a halt of its own accord, the Soviets had been able to re-establish a continuous line.

This was no new strategy. Russians had done the same thing when Napoleon of France invaded in 1812, and when Charles II of Sweden invaded in 1709. Theirs was a strategy that traded space for time: waiting for the onset of winter and mud to destroy the enemy's troops, supplies and morale, and for the enemy to be ground down by distance and hardship, Russians could then attack with a fair expectation of success. The plan had failed in the First World War when

Tsarist Russia collapsed in revolution. There was now a real fear among the Soviet commanders that Russia's traditional strategy would once again fail in the face of German organization and German arms.

It was for this reason that Stalin put so much emphasis on the need for offensive action at every opportunity. Being advised by his generals to stand on the defensive in the summer of 1943 went against his instincts. Nevertheless he went along with the plan, though not without some anxious moments.

Kursk tank trap

The Kursk salient was transformed in the spring of 1943 as the Soviets sought to turn it into a gigantic tank trap. Their aim was simply to destroy the panzers of the German Army in massive numbers. To achieve this Zhukov appointed three of his key commanders.

The northern half of the salient was held by the Central Front under General Konstantin Rokossovsky. The Soviet Red Army was organized into a series of 'fronts', each of which contained a number of separate armies. They were therefore analogous to the German army groups, though often smaller.

This Central Front was composed of the 4th, 13th, 48th, 60th, 65th and 70th Armies, plus the 2nd Tank Army and the

Opposite: Nicolai Vatutin (right), commander of the Voronezh Front, and Konstantin Rokossovsky, commander of the Central Front, meet during the Battle of Kursk. Co-operation between the two senior commanders was essential to the Soviet victory.

16th Air Army. Together these units had 711,500 men, 1,785 tanks, 12,400 guns and 1,050 aircraft. The 30-km (19-mile) stretch of front line where the German attack was expected was held by the 13th Army, with the 2nd Tank Army behind it. To its right was the 48th Army and to its left the 70th Army. The 65th and 60th Armies were even further to the left, holding the nose of the salient. The 4th Army was held back in reserve.

Rokossovsky was an unusual figure in the Red Army. He had been born in 1896 in Warsaw when Poland was a part of the Tsarist Empire. His family was from the minor Polish nobility, which had little love for Russia and even less for communism. When the First World War broke out, Rokossovsky joined the Russian cavalry and rose to become a sergeant. When the Russian Revolution occurred, he joined the Bolshevik Red Army and by 1921 was commanding a regiment in the Russian Civil War. He subsequently fought in both Mongolia and China, achieving high command.

Rokossovsky's career was brutally cut short in 1937 when he was arrested during Stalin's Great Purge. The cause of his arrest seems to have been his friendship years earlier with Marshal Vasily Blyukher, who had just been arrested on trumped-up charges of spying for Japan. Rokossovsky was accused of being a Japanese spy, a Polish spy and a saboteur, and of meeting known traitors. Despite being regularly beaten up and tortured, he refused to sign a confession. He was found guilty by a secret court anyway and thrown into prison.

In March 1940, Rokossovsky was suddenly released without any explanation and returned to his rank and position within the Red Army. He performed well during the early months of the war, especially during the defence of Moscow, and in 1942 played a key role in the destruction of the German 6th Army at Stalingrad. It was because of his fighting abilities that Zhukov put Rokossovsky in command of the Central Front. Stalin's views on the subject are not recorded.

Voronezh and Steppe fronts

Compared to Rokossovsky, Nikolai Fyodorovich Vatutin, who commanded the Voronezh Front holding the southern half of the salient, was classic Red Army material. Under his command Vatutin had the 6th and 7th Guards Armies, the 38th, 40th and 69th Armies, the 1st Tank Army and the 2nd Air Army. At this date the composition of a Guards army was identical

Opposite: A typical Red Army formation of infantry in close escort with T-34 tanks advances on the Voronezh Front near Belgorod. The combination was intended to combine the hitting power of tanks with the flexibility of infantry.

to that of a conventional army, and there was no distinction in the recruitment or training either; in fact the designation of 'Guards' was merely an honorary one. If a unit performed particularly well in action it could be given the title of Guards by the Soviet defence minister. In theory this conferred some form of elite status – and men serving in Guards armies had a distinctive cap badge – but in practice it is hard to see any real difference between a Guards army and normal army. These units totalled 626,000 men with 1,700 tanks, 9,700 guns and 881 aircraft.

Held in reserve to the east was the Steppe Front. This was composed of just three armies – the 5th Guards Army, 27th, 47th and 53rd Armies, the 5th Guards Tank Army and 5th Air Army. This force totalled 573,000 men with 1,650 tanks, 9,200 guns and 560 aircraft.

The Steppe Front was commanded by Ivan Konev, who came from Russian peasant stock, like Vatutin. He had been working as a lumberjack when the Revolution broke out and he joined

the Red Army. Although barely educated, Konev proved to be a talented commander who had a sound understanding of how to use artillery in action. His career was helped by his friend-ship with Kliment Voroshilov, who in 1921 was elected to the Central Committee of the Communist Party of the Soviet Union and became a trusted confidant of Stalin. He fought a number of defensive or rearguard actions during 1941 and 1942, displaying resourcefulness and ability. It was for this reason that he was chosen to command the reserve at Kursk.

Konev took seriously the art that the Russians called *maskirovka*, a term that could be translated variously as camou-flage or deception, but which really means both. So skilled was he at this that the Germans had no idea that his Steppe Front was anywhere near Kursk.

Defence in depth

These large forces were given months to prepare to meet the German offensive, and made great use of the time. The Soviets opted for a 'defence in depth' concept. From previous bitter experience they knew that once through Red Army defences and into open country, the German panzers would speed up and spread out to disrupt supply lines, destroy communications and generally disrupt the organization of the Red Army – not to mention spreading death and destruction everywhere they went. They had been able to do this in the past because then the Soviets had been forced to hold a wide front and so had been able to put in place only a thin defence at any given point.

Now the tank-destroying potential of the Red Army was deployed densely and in depth. The first obstacle the Germans had to overcome was an area of open land regularly swept by machine-gun fire and artillery. The purpose of this area was to stop German patrols reaching the minefields that lay beyond.

The minefields were extensive, deep and dense. The purpose of the mines was not so much to kill Germans – though that would be useful – as to slow them down. The Germans knew that there would be minefields, though not how large they would be, and so could be relied upon to send forward combat engineers to clear the mines ahead of the panzers. The panzers, meanwhile, would either be kept waiting just in front of the minefields, or would motor through the few gaps in them. Either way, Soviet artillery batteries were previously zeroed in on those areas to inflict damage on the panzers.

Interspersed among the minefields were vast earthworks consisting of deep ditches backed by towering mounds constructed from the earth dug out of the ditch. These were of a shape and size so that no tank could get over them. Like the minefields, they were designed to slow the panzers and funnel them into killing zones.

Behind the minefields came the anti-tank guns. These were dug in and well camouflaged, making them difficult to see for a tank commander peering ahead from his turret. Soviet anti-tank guns were organized in groups of half a dozen, positioned so that each gun could cover the approaches to its fellows in a mutually supporting network of fire. They were not to open fire while the panzers were working through the minefields – heavier artillery placed further back did that – but to wait until the panzers were at close range when their fire would be at its most destructive.

Infantry in wait

Interspersed among the anti-tank guns were infantry units occupying trenches and dug-outs that would not have been out of place on the Somme in 1916. Most of these men were there to tackle the German infantry that was expected to advance alongside the panzers, but others were there to take on the panzers themselves. These men were equipped with petrol bombs and grenades. Their task was to hide in their trenches until the panzers had passed over them, literally, and then leap out to detonate grenades on the panzers' vulnerable tracks or hurl petrol bombs on to the engine outlets so that the spreading pool of flaming petrol would enter the engine block and render it useless.

Needless to say this was hazardous work, all the more so because the panzergrenadier infantry that accompanied the tanks were there specifically to kill such men. The panzer crews themselves were aware of the danger, so they routinely slewed around when crossing trenches in order to collapse the walls and bury alive anyone within. Nevertheless, the tactic could occasionally be successful and since Red Army commanders did not mind accepting heavy casualties it was one with which that they persisted.

Behind the anti-tank guns and infantry lurked the Soviet tanks. Some of these were placed in previously dug scoops in the ground so that only their turrets showed, while others were roaming freely over the landscape to surge forwards at any German panzers that got past the anti-tank guns.

The vast majority of Soviet tanks were of the T-34 model. Present in much smaller numbers was the 47-tonne KV-1 tank.

This heavy tank carried a 76 mm cannon as its main gun, plus two machine-guns. At 110 mm (4½ inches) thick, the armour was impressive and made this tank proof against many German weapons. However, it was notoriously slow and unmanoeuv rable, and was prone to break down without warning.

Air support

Throughout the Soviet defences were men with radios who were in touch with the main command centre for the aircraft squadrons active in the area. These men could radio for air support if the German attack appeared to be gaining the upper hand.

By this date the Soviet ground-attack aircraft used in this role were much improved on those with which they had started the war. The Ilyushin Il-2 was being produced in vast numbers – so many that it was to be the most produced aircraft of the war. It could carry up to 600 kg (1,320 lb) of bombs and had a pair of 20 mm cannons in underwing pods. What really made the Il-2 a noteworthy aircraft, however, was the fact that the engine and pilot's seat were surrounded by 13-mm (½-inch) armour plate that was proof against rifle and machine-gun bullets, and even the glancing blows of anti-aircraft rounds. This made the aircraft highly resilient to ground fire – though it was vulnerable to enemy fighters on account of its slow speed and poor manoeuvrability. Also useful for ground attack was the Pe-2, which was faster and more nimble, but could carry less weaponry.

The Tupolev Tu-2 was a more conventional bomber which could carry 3,000 kg (6,600 lb) of bombs over some 1,600 km (1,000 miles) or so. The Tu-2 was not seen much over the

Nikolai Vatutin (1901–44)

Vatutin was born in 1901 into a family of Russian peasants, joined the Communist Party as a teenager and signed up for the Red Army at the first opportunity. During the Russian Civil War he fought against the Ukrainian separatists with exceptional brutality and tenacity, ensuring their defeat. He then transferred to the military staff, and was teaching at the military academy when Stalin's Great Purge of 1936–8 began. Vatutin's orthodox Communist beliefs and peasant background spared him in the Great Purge, and indeed smoothed his path to rapid promotion basking in Stalin's favour.

When the war broke out, Vatutin quickly proved himself a skilled commander. He is widely credited with saving Leningrad, but then made a mess of a counter-offensive and lost 60 per cent of his men in little over a week of fighting. In the Stalingrad campaign he successfully halted a German attack on Voronezh, then later led the advance to Kharkov. He was given command of the southern half of the Kursk salient in March 1943 as the Stavka came to the conclusion that the Germans would attack there.

After Kursk, Vatutin commanded the Soviet forces in southern Russia. In these months, he inflicted defeats on Manstein, but also suffered more than one setback at his hands. By early 1944, Vatutin was commanding Soviet forces in the Ukraine. On 28 February he was driving near Mylyatin when his car was stopped by locals who had not forgotten his actions in the Ukraine back in 1923. They shot Vatutin and, although his guards fought them off, he died of his wounds six weeks later.

Nikolai Vatutin, the Red Army commander whose forces were badly mauled by the Germans at Kharkov in February 1943, but who recovered in time for Kursk.

battlefield, but was used more often to attack German supply lines or communications further back.

Effective as these bombers could be, the main weak link proved to be the radios. The radios of the ground troops could not communicate directly with those of the airmen but had to be routed through specialist communications centres. This resulted in unavoidable delays and misunderstandings that often saw Soviet aircraft attacking Soviet troops.

Having constructed this deep web of interlocking and mutually supportive weaponry in a defence line along the stretch of front where the Germans were expected to attack, the Soviets build a second identical line behind the first. A third line of defence was in the process of construction when the Germans finally began their offensive. Taken together, the Soviet defences were carefully constructed and imposing in strength.

It was against these defences that the German army was about to launch its combined might.

Chapter 5

COUNTDOWN

The German order of battle was finally decided upon in an operational instruction issued by OKH on 14 June 1943. There was to be a further delay before the fighting began due to the desire to get as many Tiger and Panther tanks into the front line as possible, but this did not affect the disposition of units.

Von Kluge's Army Group Centre was responsible not only for the thrust from the north, but also for applying pressure to the nose of the salient and guarding the northern flank of the armoured punch against any attempted counter-attack.

To hold the western edge of the salient, Kluge used the 2nd Army commanded by Walter Weiss. This force consisted of nine infantry divisions with supporting artillery but no panzers or self-propelled guns. Weiss was in his late fifties in 1943 and had spent his entire military career from 1908 onwards as a competent officer of infantry. He had served in Poland and France, and in Russia since 1941. He had shown himself to be hard-working and reliable, but had no major victories to his credit. He was clearly a commander who could hold an unimportant sector.

Guarding the northern flank of the main force was the 2nd Panzer Army. This title was a complete misnomer because the force had no panzer units. It was composed instead of 12 infantry divisions and one division of panzergrenadiers. The panzergrenadiers consisted of infantry mounted in trucks, with armoured cars and self-propelled guns. The Army was a strong one, but it was not a panzer force.

The main strike force was composed of the 9th Army. This was just as misleading a name as that of the 2nd Panzer Army, for the 9th Army was packed with armoured vehicles. Only two of the five corps in the 9th Army were conventional infantry corps of four infantry divisions each, all the other corps being to some extent mechanized.

Panzer strength

The main fighting strength of 9th Army was the XLVII Panzer Corps and XLI Panzer Corps. The stronger of these was the XLVII Panzer Corps, which had three panzer divisions and one infantry division. It was commanded by General Joachim Lemelsen, in many ways a typical career officer of the German army.

Lemelsen was born in Berlin in 1888, the son of an army officer, and joined the army at the age of 18. He fought through the First World War, ending with the Iron Cross, First Class and Second Class, and the rank of captain. He remained in the army after the war, at first specializing in infantry-artillery co-operation but later taking an interest in panzer tactics. He commanded an infantry division in Poland in 1939, and a panzer division in France in 1940.

Lemelsen took command of the XLVII Panzer Corps in time for the invasion of Russia. He and his new corps played a lead role in the panzer actions of 1941, but were less active in 1942. Lemelsen made repeated and strong protests about the activities of the SS and other units in rear areas. On one occasion he wrote a long letter of protest direct to OKH that included the words, 'I am repeatedly finding out about the shooting of prisoners, defectors or deserters, carried out in an irresponsible, senseless and criminal manner. This is murder.' The protests fell on deaf ears, but Lemelsen was not alone among army officers to be disgusted by the actions of the Nazis, though he took no part in the various schemes by different army officers to assassinate Hitler.

For Kursk, Lemelsen had 331 tanks and self-propelled guns, plus 232 artillery pieces. Of his tanks, 45 were Tigers.

The slightly less impressive XLI Panzer Corps was commanded by General Josef Harpe. Like Lemelsen, Harpe was an old-school Prussian army officer who had fought through the First World War in the infantry and been highly decorated for courage. In 1931 he adopted the false name of 'Hacker' so that he was free to write innovative articles and studies on panzer tactics without being challenged by fellow officers. These were not so influential as those of Guderian, but they did form an element in the gradual defining of *blitzkrieg* theory in the German army. After serving as the commander of the Panzer Training School, Harpe took up command of the XLI Panzer Corps in July 1942.

Under his command Harpe had one panzer and two infantry divisions, with 304 tanks and self-propelled guns, plus 234 guns. Among the self-propelled guns in the XLI Panzer Corps were 83 Elefant self-propelled guns, out of 89 that had been built by this date. Great things were expected of this weapon with its powerful 88 mm gun.

In addition to these two panzer corps, Model had XX Corps, made up of four infantry divisions under Rudolf von Roman. Model also had XLVI Corps, which had four infantry divisions plus nine tanks and 31 assault guns. The XLVI Corps was commanded by Hans Zorn, one of the most highly decorated officers in the German army. A third infantry corps, the XXIII, with just three divisions, was under the command of Johannes Freissner. Freissner had been in the army since 1911, but had enjoyed only slow promotion. He achieved general rank only in 1940 and took over his corps in January 1943.

In addition to these forces, Model held back in reserve two panzer divisions and one of panzergrenadiers. These forces were under his own personal command.

Model's plan of assault

It should be remembered that Model had been opposed to the *Zitadelle* offensive for some months, believing that the Soviet defences were so strong that heavy German casualties were inevitable. His assault plan was, therefore, unconventional and designed to minimize casualties among his troops.

Model deduced from a study of aerial photographs that the Soviet defences were designed to ensnare and destroy his panzer forces, which was exactly what Zhukov was planning. Therefore Model decided not to lead his attack with panzers but with infantry forces, closely supported by artillery and with heavy Luftwaffe cover. If the Soviets were expecting panzers, Model was going to send them infantry.

This novel form of attack was, in fact, very close to the

Von Kluge (left) discusses the progress of the 9th Army's offensive with its commander General Walter Model several days after the Kursk offensive began. Together the two men decided to call off the main attack on their front.

massively successful storm-trooper tactics that had achieved so much for the German army in 1918. Highly skilled teams of infantry would push forward, worming their way between enemy strongpoints and cutting them off from reinforcement before calling down heavy artillery or air bombardment to pound them out of existence. Anti-tank weapons would be next to useless against infantry, though they could be expected to take a toll on the assault guns that came up in support.

Having broken through the Soviet defences with infantry, Model planned then to unleash his panzers, sending them racing ahead to Kursk to spread destruction and panic in their wake. If all went well, the panzers would be in Kursk ten days after the first attack was launched.

In Model's favour was the element of surprise and the superb levels of co-operation between different units in which the Germans excelled. Infantry commanders could talk directly to artillery battery commanders over radio to call in barrages, and could speak to Stuka commanders to ensure that the famed pinpoint accuracy of the feared dive-bombers hit the enemy where it would hurt most.

The 6th Air Fleet of the Luftwaffe that would be providing air support to Model was commanded by Robert Ritter von Greim. Von Greim was a successful fighter pilot in the First World War, serving alongside another dashing pilot named Hermann Goering. By the end of the war Greim had shot down 28 Allied aircraft and had been awarded a clutch of high decorations for valour and leadership.

When the German air force was disbanded by the Allies in 1919, Greim worked for a while as a civilian pilot, and in 1921 met aspiring politician Adolf Hitler. He was then hired by the Chinese government to establish and command a new Chinese air force. By 1933 he was back in Germany and had been contacted by Hitler and Goering with an offer to help build up the new Luftwaffe in the position of Head of Research. When the war broke out he took up a combat command and so was active in the invasions of Poland and Norway as well as the Battle of Britain.

Counting against Model's chances of success was the quality of his infantry divisions. Only one of Model's infantry divisions was of the top quality – assault troops equipped and trained to the highest offensive level. No less than four were of the lowest standard allowed in the front line; they were not supposed to be used in offensive operations, only in defensive positions.

It was, even Model would have admitted, a risky plan. But it was the best he had. Time would tell how robust it was when faced by Soviet defences.

Manstein's outlook

On the southern flank of the Kursk salient, Manstein was preparing his own plans for the attack. For his assault, Manstein had a more powerful force and decided to use it quite differently.

Manstein handed the task of the offensive to the 4th Panzer Army under Hermann Hoth; the other three armies of the Army Group South were infantry units assigned to remain on the defensive on the line south of Kursk down to the Black Sea. The 4th Panzer Army was the most powerful army the Germans ever mustered, and Hoth was the man to lead it.

Under his command, Hoth had three very different corps. The LII Corps was composed of three infantry divisions and led by Eugen Ott, a senior commander with a solid if undistinguished record.

The XLVIII Panzer Corps was composed of two panzer divisions, the 3rd and 11th, plus the Grossdeutschland Panzergrenadier Division and one infantry division. This corps was led by Otto von Knobelsdorff, a talented commander who had spent most of his career in panzer units.

The second panzer corps in Hoth's army was the II SS Panzer Corps, composed of the 1st SS Panzergrenadier Division Leibstandarte SS Adolf Hitler, 2nd SS Panzergrenadier Division Das Reich and 3rd SS Panzergrenadier Division Totenkopf. This was an elite corps, under the command of the distinguished and highly regarded Paul Hausser.

Hausser was born into an old army family in 1880, served with distinction through the First World War and retired in 1931 with the rank of major general. He then joined the Stalheim, a 500,000-strong organization of army veterans that had as its main political aim the overturning of the Versailles Treaty that had ended the First World War. After Hitler came to power the Stalheim was closed down due to its anti-Nazi policies and some of its leaders were thrown into prison.

Instead of being arrested, however, Hausser was invited to join the SS-VT. This was a unit within the SS made up of retired soldiers that was to undertake tasks given them by

Hitler, mostly consisting of guarding Nazi Party property or senior figures. At this date the SS formed a part of the Nazi Party, but unlike all other civilian organizations its members were allowed to carry guns in public.

In 1939 Hausser was given command of the SS panzergrenadier divisions, and so became the founder of the Waffen-SS. This anomalous organization was a uniquely Nazi unit. Officially the Waffen-SS (the name means 'armed bodyguard') was a part of the Nazi Party. Recruitment was open only to Germans – though this included ethnically German men from outside Germany itself. This kept it racially pure, in line with Nazi ideology.

The men of the Waffen-SS were members of and employees of the Nazi Party with no official links to the regular German army. Despite this, the Waffen-SS had an organization that mimicked that of the army, with identical ranks and command structures. It was also equipped as was the army, with the same tanks, assault guns, rifles and other equipment.

The control of the Waffen-SS was officially in the hands of Heinrich Himmler, head of the SS and Gestapo. For operational matters, however, the Waffen-SS came under the orders of the regular army command structure. The Waffen-SS therefore occupied the strange position of being armed as if it were part of the army and coming under army orders, and yet not being a part of the army.

Within the Germany army, the Waffen-SS enjoyed a reputation as being an elite and highly effective force. However, they were also recognized to be hardline Nazi Party acolytes who were known to carry out atrocities and barbaric acts that regular army officers viewed with distaste and concern. The Waffen-SS were also prone to be rash and over-aggressive in action and more than once had got into trouble by advancing too far and too fast for safety.

'Army Detachment Kempf'

Also included in the 4th Panzer Army was the 'Army Detachment Kempf', an unusual grouping of three corps which was named after its commander, Werner Kempf. It had been formed in February 1943 out of the shattered remnants of a number of different units that had been broken up or disorganized during the fighting around Stalingrad. Kempf welded these units together into a cohesive fighting group that took his name. In the months after it formed, Army Detachment Kempf had seen its component parts reinforced, reorganized and re-equipped. Ordinarily this process would have the informal designation of an Army Detachment named after its commander replaced by a regular title and formalized command structure. That this never happened may have had as much to do with Hitler's whim as anything else.

By the time of the Kursk offensive, Army Detachment Kempf was composed of three corps. The III Panzer Corps contained the 6th, 7th and 19th Panzer Divisions plus the 168th Infantry Division under the command of Hermann Breith. General Breith had won the Iron Cross, both First Class and Second Class, in the First World War as an infantry officer, then gained the clasp to both classes in 1939 when commanding panzers during the invasion of Poland. He was wounded in June 1940 during the invasion of France, but was fit for duty again in 1942 when he was given command of 3rd Panzer Division, moving up to corps command level in January 1943.

Kempf's second corps was the XI Army Corps, composed of the 106th and 320th Infantry Divisions. The commander of XI Army Corps, Erhard Raus, had an unusual background for a *Wehrmacht* commander. He had been born in 1889 in the town of Wolframitz, now Olbramovice in the Czech Republic but then part of the Austro-Hungarian Empire. He joined the Austrian army in 1909 and saw considerable action with the uniquely Austrian bicycle light infantry. He remained in the Austrian army after the First World War.

When Germany annexed Austria in 1938 the Austrian army was merged with that of Germany, and so Raus came to serve in the German army. He served at first in a succession of staff positions, but in May 1941 he took command of a brigade of motorized infantry and thereafter his rise was rapid. He led the spearhead trying to break through to Stalingrad in December 1942 and was of the opinion that he could have got to Stalingrad and saved the 6th Army if he had been given enough petrol and ammunition – ignoring the fact that he had been given all that there was.

Completing Army Detachment Kempf was the XLII Corps of three infantry divisions under Franz Mattenklott. His background was fairly conventional. Born in Prussia, he joined the army in 1903 at the age of 18 and gradually worked his way up through the ranks of the infantry officers. The climb was slow, Mattenklott not achieving general rank until the age of 53. When the Second World War broke out, he was leading a division on the French frontier, and he remained there, largely inactive, while the Polish and Scandinavian campaigns unfolded. Even when the Germans invaded France, Mattenklott had only a limited role, watching the French Maginot Line rather than taking any offensive actions.

Mattenklott's first real taste of battle in high command came during the 1941 invasion of Greece when his infantry broke through the fortified mountain positions known as the Metaxas Line. Later that year he led his men into Russia, and played a distinguished role in the siege of Sevastopol. He then commanded rear area troops through most of 1942 and early 1943. Mattenklott was actually on leave when he was hurriedly summoned back to Russia for the Kursk offensive, and arrived only a couple of days before the battle began.

Von Richthofen in support

The air support for Manstein's forces came from 4th Air Fleet, commanded by the charismatic Wolfram Freiherr von Richthofen. Von Richthofen was the inheritor of a famous name, as his cousin had been Manfred Freiherr von Richthofen, the 'Red Baron' of First World War fame. After a successful career in engineering, von Richthoven joined the Luftwaffe in 1933. There he championed the cause of light- and dive-bombers working in close co-operation with ground troops and is credited with having perfected the air component of *blitzkrieg* tactics. He fought in nearly every campaign of the war, achieving far more than anyone had expected during the Stalingrad campaign, and by July 1943 was perhaps the most admired officer in the Luftwaffe.

The more Hoth and Manstein studied the plans for the Kursk offensive sent to them from OKH, the less they liked them. The plans called for the 4th Panzer Army to batter a way through the Soviet defences along a 50-km (30-mile) front between Belgorod and Gertsovka. Once through, the panzers were to push directly north to Kursk to meet Model's 9th Army coming south.

However, the countryside around Oboyan, half way to Kursk, was hilly and forested – far from ideal for panzers. Moreover, Hoth and Manstein thought that the Soviets were likely to have a large reserve force somewhere to the east. This, they thought, would be brought up as soon as the panzers broke through. If the Germans went directly north, the Soviets would smash into their right flank with potentially disastrous results.

A new plan

Hoth and Manstein quietly tore up the plans from OKH. Their new plan saw them attacking in the same place as OKH suggested, but once through the Soviet defences they would turn north-east instead of continuing north. This would take the panzers around the eastern flank of the forested hills and keep them in open country, where the German panzers would enjoy an advantage over any new Soviet reserves. Hoth guessed that the battle against the reserves would probably take place somewhere near Prokhorovka, a small town that had grown up around a junction on the Moscow–Kharkov railway.

Turning to the operational detail of the assault, Manstein and Hoth decided to use their armour in the early stages of the battle to blast a path through the dense defences. Manstein in particular was frustrated by the fact that he was being asked to fight a battle of attrition in a compact area instead of using the speed of his panzers to manoeuvre and outflank the enemy, but once the decision had been taken to attack at Kursk he felt he had to do his best.

Hoth and Manstein summoned Hausser and outlined to him how the SS panzer units were to form the initial fighting punch of the offensive. Once Hausser was made fully aware both of the plans sent from OKH and of the strength and nature of the Soviet defences, he became as wary of the battle to come as his commanders.

'Our success will demand all of our talent, experience and ruthlessness,' Hausser noted after the meeting. 'The SS are but one small part of the complex machine for this operation. We have put our faith in armour and must pray that that faith has not been misplaced.' It was hardly a clarion call of confidence in victory.

As the preparations for the assault dragged on, some of the German High Command began to wonder if the Soviets really knew what was coming or not. There were few, if any, air attacks on the roads being used by supply columns heading for the Kursk area, and none at all on the areas in which the vast numbers of men and panzers were gathering. If the Soviets had known about this build-up of resources, the most usual thing would have been for them to bomb them. Even the stores and assembly areas right up near the front lines and within range of heavy Soviet artillery were largely left alone. Soviet reconnaissance aircraft did not seem to be making much effort to get over the German lines and find out what was going on.

The truth was, of course, that the Soviets were so confident of the information they were receiving from the British and from their own spies that they believed that they knew exactly what was happening. Indeed, they did not wish to put the Germans off from attacking at Kursk for they were confident that they could defeat whatever was thrown at them. It was for this reason that they made no special efforts, but instead merely continued as usual.

Partisan attacks

Something that was usual, but did cause the Germans concern, was the level of partisan activity. The operation of armed partisans in rear areas of the German-occupied lands had originated in 1941 among Red Army men cut off by the rapidly advancing panzers. They took what opportunities they could to hit at isolated German outposts and transport trucks.

By the spring of 1943, however, the partisan groups were supplied and organized from a special section of the Stavka. The various units were given their orders with a view to supporting the Red Army as much as disrupting the Germans. As with most Soviet activity, the lives of those involved were not a high priority, nor was the well-being of the local civilians.

Partisan groups were expected to find their own supplies, even if that meant getting them off the local Soviet farmers. Given that the Germans had already impounded what they saw as surplus food stocks, the partisans did not always find local farmers willing to hand over food. In many areas the partisans took food and other supplies by force, and shot anyone who objected.

The local population also suffered from German retaliation. The Germans took the view that partisans could operate only if they gathered food, supplies and shelter from the local population. In the German view, therefore, the local civilians who sheltered partisans were as guilty as the partisans themselves. With typcal Nazi brutality, the Germans made little effort to find which – if any – civilians had assisted a partisan group. Instead a number of local civilians were rounded up and shot whenever a partisan attack took place.

It is impossible to be certain of the numbers involved because neither the partisans nor the Germans kept very careful records. It is thought, however, that something around half a million civilians in German-occupied areas were killed as a result of partisan activity and German reprisals.

As the weeks counted down to the German offensive at Kursk, the Soviets directed more and more partisan activity into the areas through which supplies for the German units at Kursk would pass. Care was taken to make sure that the build-up of effort was neither obvious nor great enough for the Germans to become suspicious.

Nevertheless von Kluge, at least, recognized the detrimental effect of the partisans. In a way he had no choice. In the two months leading up to the fighting at Kursk the partisans blew up 44 bridges and sabotaged 300 trains in the Army Group Centre area. Von Kluge detached five divisions from the front to sweep his rear areas, seeking to pin down and annihilate partisan groups. They achieved much, but could not root out all the partisan groups.

The Eastern Front as at 1 July 1943.

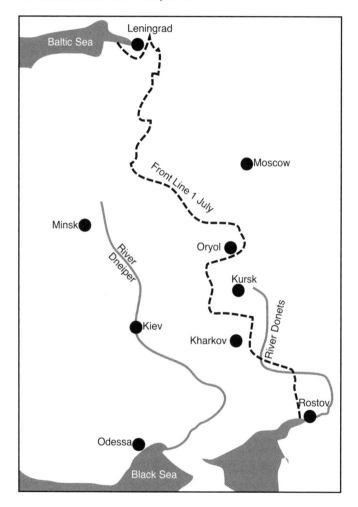

Hermann Hoth (1885–1971)

The son of an army officer, Hermann Hoth joined the German army in 1903. He entered the First World War as an infantry captain, won the Iron Cross (both classes) and emerged with a reputation for personal courage and a flair for innovative methods.

After the war he opted to remain in the much-reduced German army, where he reached the rank of general in 1935 and was given the 18th Infantry Division to command. He was later appointed to the XV Motorized Corps, and was commanding that unit when war broke out; his handling of the fast-moving unit ensured that he was at the head of a panzer corps for the invasion of France in 1940. Among his subordinate commanders in France was Erwin Rommel, and together the two men earned a reputation for masterful use of panzers in action.

Hoth led a panzer group in the early stages of the invasion of Russia, taking over 4th Panzer Army in June 1942. He led the 4th Panzer Army on the drive south-east towards the Caucasus with skill, though his forces were ultimately unsuccessful. It was Hoth who led the attempt to break through to Stalingrad in December 1942. The effort failed, but again Hoth showed his skill in commanding panzers.

After Kursk, Hoth retained command of the 4th Panzer Army until Hitler decided he would make a good scapegoat for the defeats suffered by the Germans. Hoth was sacked in November 1943. He was recalled in April 1945, just days before the war ended. In 1948 he was found guilty of war crimes at Nuremburg and sentenced to 15 years, though he was released after serving half his sentence.

Hermann Hoth commanded the 4th Panzer Army at Kursk.

Misleading intelligence

On 1 July 1943 Hitler summoned his senior Eastern Front commanders to the forward headquarters of OKH, known as the Wolf's Lair (*Wolfsschanze*). Hitler told his commanders, 'I have decided to fix the start date for *Zitadelle* on the 5th of July.'

The decision was based on a plethora of intelligence reports that Hitler then outlined to his generals. These reports gave an accurate picture of German strength and resouces. Mustering to take part in the attack were 780,900 men, 2,928 tanks and self-propelled guns and 7,417 pieces of artillery. Air support was to come from 2,110 aircraft.

The Germans estimated that the Soviets had in the Kursk area about 1 million men, 1,500 tanks and some 20,000 guns. The estimate, though based on careful staff work and analysis of all the available evidence, was hopelessly wrong. In fact the Soviets had 1,900,000 men, 5,128 tanks and 31,000 guns. In large part the discrepancy was caused by the failure of the Germans to locate and identify the Steppe Front under Ivan Konev that was being held in reserve far to the east, but most was due to good camouflage by the Soviets.

In contrast to the poor quality of the German intelligence, that of the Soviets was excellent. Less than 36 hours after Hitler made his announcement, the Lucy spy ring had sent a signal to the Stavka telling it that the German offensive would begin within seven days. Stalin authorized that the armies around Kursk be put on high alert. Zhukov left the Stavka and moved in at the headquarters of Rokossovsky on the Central Front which was holding the northern edge of the Kursk salient.

Preliminary maneouvre

The first move came as a surprise to nearly everyone, except those immediately involved. Just after dawn on 4 July the Grossdeutschland Division of the XLVIII Panzer Corps in Hoth's 4th Panzer Army suddenly surged forward. Undetected by Soviet patrols, the German sappers had the night before cleared paths through the minefields so that the advance could take place without delay. Within a few hours the villages of Gertsovka and Butovo were captured. The villages were empty, all civilians having been cleared out of the area by the Red Army several days beforehand.

The German advance stopped as suddenly as it had begun. The purpose had been to grab some high ground that gave German artillery spotters a clear view over Soviet defences in the area. If the Soviets had been in any doubt that the battle was imminent, this short advance dispelled the idea.

The great Battle of Kursk was about to begin.

Chapter 6

THE ASSAULT

At 2 am on 5 July German officers all along the front opened sealed envelopes that they had been given and found inside a message from Adolf Hitler himself to be read out to the troops.

'Soldiers of the Reich!

'This day you are to take part in an offensive of such importance that the whole future of the war may depend on its outcome. More than anything else, your victory will show the whole world that resistance to the power of the German Army is hopeless.

'This powerful strike, which you will direct at the Soviet armies this morning, must shake them to their roots. The German homeland has placed its deepest trust in you.'

In fact the offensive had already begun. All along the front where the German attack was to be launched, teams of sappers and engineers had crept forwards into the darkness. Their task was to clear the minefields and cut the barbed wire that formed the first line of the Soviet defences. In many ways, this made the opening stages of the Battle of Kursk more like the Western Front of the First World War than anything that had so far been seen on the Eastern Front.

The Eastern Front as at 5 July 1943.

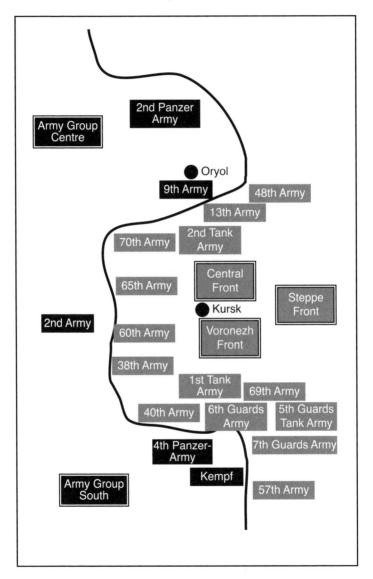

Inevitably some of the Germans had been seen by Soviet defenders. Machine-gun fire and mortars lashed out to stop the German work. German weaponry opened up in retaliation, seeking to zero in on and destroy the Soviet defenders. A little after midnight a German engineer was captured while marking a safe path for panzers to follow. Under questioning he revealed that the attack would begin at 3.30 am.

Soviet attack

As soon as Zhukov heard this news he ordered that the long-planned Soviet bombardment should commence at 2 am. This was the first indication that the Germans had that the Soviets knew much about the offensive plan at all. It came as a nasty shock, and Manstein in particular drew the conclusion that their plans had somehow become known to the enemy.

The bombardment was heavy but short. Thousands of Soviet shells crashed down into the areas where the Germans were expected to be gathering to push through gaps in the mine-fields and tank-proof embankments. In fact, many of the Soviet shells fell on empty fields as the German units had not yet got to their jumping off positions.

The bombardment had, however, inflicted casualties and had churned up the ground over which men and wheeled vehicles were supposed to advance. The German attack was postponed to 4 am, but otherwise it mostly began as planned.

At 4 am, therefore, the German artillery opened up. If the Soviets had wasted much of their fire on fields and woods, the German fire was much more accurate – though not necessarily more destructive. In the course of the next hour the German artillery fired more shells than they had done during the entire invasion of France in 1940. The plan was to knock out Soviet front-line artillery, bury infantry in their trenches and disrupt communications systems.

Meanwhile, dawn crept up over the steppes, and with it came the Soviet air force. The Soviets had put considerable efforts into locating the Luftwaffe's forward airfields. Spies had been infiltrated through the lines to scour the countryside for the temporary facilities and cleared land that marked an airfield in the forward area. Now the Soviet air force was coming in at low level and first light to devastate the Luftwaffe before it could enter the fray.

The reason the Soviets were determined to destroy German aircraft on the ground was simple. The German air force was the dominant arm in the German bombardment plan. While other armies relied upon artillery and self-propelled guns, the Germans used light-bombers or dive-bombers to pound the enemy positions on the battlefield. If those bombers could be destroyed the Germans would have to rely on their artillery instead – and they had considerably fewer cannon than the Soviets.

The Germans had not been expecting the Soviet strike, but they detected it on their radar screens in time for all the German aircraft to be airborne by the time the Soviet aircraft arrived over the German bases. German anti-aircraft guns ringed their bases and put up a heavy barrage as the enemy aircraft came in to attack. Those Soviet pilots who escaped the ground fire found themselves attacked by Luftwaffe fighters that had been circling overhead looking for an opportunity to dive down with guns blazing.

Within less than an hour 176 of the 407 attacking aircraft had been shot down, with many more limping home damaged. The Luftwaffe had lost just 26 aircraft in the fighting.

Air battle

Once the Soviet surprise attack had been dealt with, the Luftwaffe returned to its designated duty of carrying out ground-attack missions to support the army as it moved forward into the Soviet defence zone. By the time the sun set that evening the Germans had flown more than 4,300 sorties.

Not all those sorties were to attack the Red Army on the ground; many were flown by fighters protecting the bombers. The Luftwaffe tactic was to place its fighters some distance away from the ground fighting to patrol high overhead and pounce on any Communist aircraft seeking to get to the combat zone. Be they bombers intending to attack German ground troops or fighters after the German bombers, the Soviets found it very difficult to get through the German fighter screen.

The Soviets flew 3,300 sorties on 5 July, but largely without success. A Soviet report related: 'While the Fascist bombers were operating almost constantly against our ground forces in the battlefield area, our aircraft were fighting mostly against enemy fighters on the approaches to the battlefield.'

Plan of battle – in the north

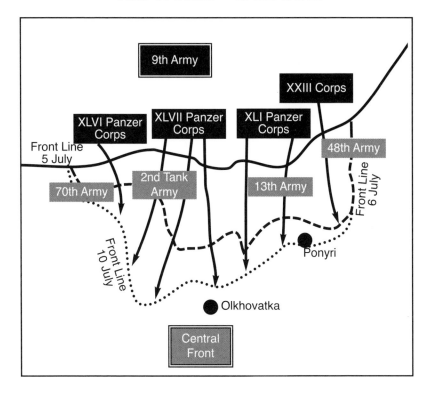

The German attack from the north.

The northern offensive was delivered by Model's 9th Army. On the right flank, to the west, was the XLVI Panzer Corps under Josef Harpe. To their left was the XLVII Panzer Corps of Joachim Lemelsen, the main armoured strength of the 9th Army. On their left was the XLI Panzer Corps of Hans Zom. On Model's left flank was XXIII Corps of Johannes Freissner.

Model had never been convinced of the wisdom of the

Zitadelle offensive, and this may have fed into his plans. He chose to lead his assault with infantry, with a small number of panzers playing a supporting role. The bulk of the panzers were held back to race forwards and exploit whatever break-through the assaulting troops could make. Indeed, only one panzer division out of six was committed to action on the first day. That 20th Panzer Division was a strong one and two extra battalions of Tigers were brought up, but even so the overall offensive was very light on armoured might.

OKH had told Model to break through by the end of the second day, and this was what Model told his senior commanders to expect. Several of them were unconvinced, and later came to believe that Model himself had not anticipated such success. Why else would he be holding the panzers so far back?

After the respective bombardments by both German and Soviet artillery, the main attack began at 5.30 am. On the left centre the 6th Infantry Division went forwards with the two battalions of Tigers. On the right centre the advance was led by the 20th Panzer and 6th Infantry Divisions. Both advances quickly ran into unexpected minefields, but these had been cleared by 8 am and the advance recommenced.

Overhead the struggle to control the air was being fought between the Luftwaffe and the Soviet air force. The numbers favoured the Soviets, but the German aircraft were more effec-tive and their pilots more experienced. Both sides concentrated on ground-attack duties, with fighters seeking to down enemy bombers. By noon it was difficult to determine who had the upper hand, though at dusk it was clear that the Germans had been the more effective of the two air forces.

The pause to clear minefields turned out to have an unexpected benefit for the Germans. A captured Soviet soldier revealed that the German bombardment had been particularly destructive in the area held by the Red Army's 81st Rifle Division. That was not an area the Germans had been intending to assault directly, but it was reasonably close to where the Tigers and 6th Infantry Division were moving forward. Those units were quickly redirected and struck the already battered Soviet riflemen at about 9 am, preceded by heavy attacks carried out by Stukas.

T-34s take on Tigers

The Soviet defences gave way and the Tigers moved forwards into the open country between the Soviet first and second defensive lines. Suddenly the Soviets sent in a force of 90 T-34 tanks. The T-34s came on fast, not pausing to find their way nor to open fire but powering forwards with as much speed as they could manage. The Soviet tank commanders had learnt the hard way that although the T-34 was a superb tank, it had its limitations in combat with the Germans. Its frontal armour was strong, though it could be destroyed by the German 88 mm gun, but the side armour of the T-34 was relatively weak and could be penetrated even by hand-held weapons wielded by the German infantry.

The aim of the T-34 tactics at this point was to get as close to the German tanks as possible so that the Soviet 76.2 mm gun could open fire at shorter range. The Soviets knew that the frontal armour of the Tiger and Panther were impervious to T-34 gunfire, but hoped that the side armour might be vulnerable. Getting close to the enemy would be dangerous, so the tanks kept on the move at high speed to make themselves more difficult to hit.

A key drawback of the T-34 was its gunsight, which gave the commander (who doubled up as gun operator) a very narrow field of view. This quickly revealed a weakness. As soon as a T-34 came under fire and the commander disappeared inside his tank he could not get a good idea of what was going on around him. It was a drawback exacerbated by the lack of a radio, meaning that one tank commander could not watch the blind spot of the next.

One German noted that: 'T-34s operated in a disorganized fashion with little co-ordination, or else tended to clump together like a hen with its chicks. Individual tank commanders lacked situational awareness due to the poor provision of vision devices and preoccupation with gunnery duties. A tank platoon would seldom be capable of engaging three separate targets, but would tend to focus on a single target selected by the platoon leader. As a result T-34 platoons lost the greater firepower of three independently operating tanks.'

While the T-34s were moving constantly, the Tigers adopted the standard German tactic of move-stop-aim-fire-move-stop-aim-fire. Compared to the Soviet tactics, this gave the Germans mobility combined with well-aimed shots. The greater visibility of the German tanks ensured that the tank commander, unhampered by the need to work the gun, could identify targets with speed and confidence.

The fighting lasted for nearly three hours. The Soviets lost 42 tanks during the fighting, while only two Tigers were knocked out. Rarely has a disparity in military hardware been so starkly demonstrated on the field of battle.

Enter the Borgward – and the Goliath

Nevertheless, the Soviet commanders were content. The fast-moving tank battle had held up the German advance long enough for Nikolai Putov, Commander of the Soviet 13th Army, to rush up his 29th Corps, with accompanying anti-tank guns, to strengthen the second line in front of the Tigers. Any chance of smashing on through the second line in a swift follow up assault had been lost to the Germans.

Nevertheless the second line had to be breached. To tackle the dense minefields that lay in front of the main Soviet defences, the Germans now brought up two revolutionary weapons.

The first and most effective of these was the Borgward IV. To the casual observer the Borgward looked rather like a small tank. It was 3.3 m (10 ft) long, 1.8 m (6 ft) wide and 1.2 m (4 ft) feet tall, had tracked wheels and was encased in armour. Closer inspection, however, showed that the Borgward had no turret and no guns. In fact this was a specialist tool of the military engineers.

The Borgward had a crew of one, who rode on it until reaching the scene of operations. The driver would then climb off and thereafter drive the vehicle by means of a radio remote-control device. The Borgward would trundle forwards at about walking pace until it had reached the minefield to be cleared. The relatively light 2.7-tonne weight of the vehicle ensured that it did not set off the mines, which were calibrated to be detonated by the weight of an 18-tonne tank. Once in what was deemed to be the most advantageous position, however, the Borgward would drop a 400-kg (880-lb) box that contained a charge of high explosives.

The operator then reversed the Borgward to a safe distance before pushing the button on the radio control panel that detonated the charge. The resulting blast and its shock waves detonated any mines within a considerable radius. The Borgward then trundled forwards once more to place a second charge. The process continued until the entire minefield had been cleared.

Good as it was, the Borgward was fairly easy to spot on the move, and made a tempting target for Soviet anti-tank gunners. Its 20-mm (¾-inch) armour was proof against bullets, but was easily smashed by armour-piercing rounds. The Germans had therefore developed what was officially named the Sd.Kfz303, though it was more widely known as the Goliath.

This vehicle was much smaller than the Borgward, being only 1.5 m (5 ft) long, 1 m (3⅓ ft) wide, 0.6 m (2 ft) tall and weighing less than 400 kg (880 lb). The Goliath was controlled by means of a wire that carried electric signals from a control box. The 650-m (2,130-ft) length of the wire effectively marked the limit that a Goliath could be sent forwards by the operator who was hiding under cover.

The Goliath carried an explosive charge that varied in size between 60 kg (130 lb) and 100 kg (220 lb). For mine-clearing duties, the Goliath was used in the same way as the Borgward, the detonation of the charge setting off the mines around it. The key difference was that the Goliath was a single-use weapon. When its charge was set off the entire vehicle was destroyed as well. Although its charge was not so powerful as that of the

Borgward, the Goliath proved more successful because it was very difficult for a Soviet gun crew to see the low-profile vehicle moving forwards and then they found it just as difficult to hit.

While the engineers were clearing the minefields to open the path for the Tigers to tackle the second line of Soviet defences, the older Panzer III and Panzer IV tanks were fanning out along the first line to take Soviet positions in flank and rear. This opened a path for German forces that had not yet broken through to advance and join in the battle for the second line of defences.

Also in action were the new Elefant self-propelled guns. In all 45 of these weapons were sent forward on 5 July, but 12 were soon out of action due to hitting mines. These promising weapons were already being found to be cumbersome in action. They were nevertheless effective in supporting the infantry of the XLI Panzer Corps as they pushed forwards towards the village of Ponyri. Those Elefants that advanced too far were, however, doomed. Any Elefant that got ahead of its supporting infantry would soon find itself surrounded by a horde of Red Army infantry armed with petrol bombs, demolition charges and even just grenades. Lacking built-in machine-guns, the Elefant crews could fight back only by opening the hatches and using the pistols and submachine-guns with which they had been issued for self-defence.

As so often, the Soviets took heavy casualties but pushed on. Their aim was to create enough confusion with grenade blasts and fires to allow some of their number to get on to the sides of the German vehicles. If petrol bombs could be detonated immediately in front of the gun mounting, the burning petrol would trickle down into the engine compartment and might, with luck, start a fire that would prove fatal to the vehicle – and the crew.

The Germans quickly learnt the vulnerability of the Elefant and some hours in the early afternoon of 5 July were spent trying to put matters right. Elefants were withdrawn, infantry pushed forwards and air strikes brought down to hit the Soviets wherever they became too adventurous. It all took time, however, and as the hours slipped away the opportunity to assault the Soviets' second line on 5 July likewise slipped away.

By the time the sun set on 5 July the Germans of Model's 9th Army were about 8–10 km (5–6 miles) into Soviet territory and in most places were through the first line of defence. This was no isolated thrust: the penetration had been achieved over a frontage of 65 km (40 miles). It was a good start for Model and seemed to justify his decision to lead with the infantry.

Southern assault

In the south, Hoth's 4th Panzer Army was advancing on a narrower front barely 50 km (30 miles) wide. In the centre was the II SS Panzer Corps, on the left was the XLVIII Panzer Corps and on the right was the III Panzer Corps. The plan, as drawn up by OKH, envisaged that the first line of Soviet defences would be broken by around noon, the second line by dusk and the third line the next day. Thereafter the 4th Panzer Army was to race north with its motorized divisions, while the infantry mopped up any undefeated Soviet positions and guarded the flanks of the advancing panzers so that they would not be cut off and surrounded.

It did not work out like that.

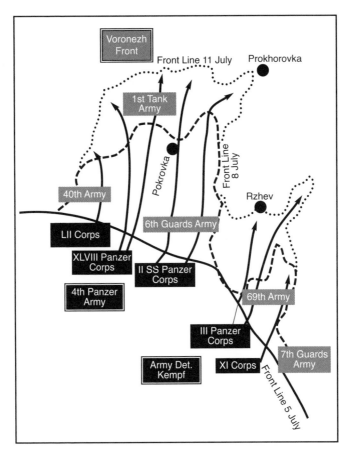

The German attack from the south.

The XLVIII Panzer Corps was spearheaded by the Grossdeutschland Panzergrenadier Division, which had 384 tanks – of which 15 were Tigers and 200 Panthers, the rest being Panzer III and Panzer IV. To the left of the Grossdeutschland was 3rd Panzer Division and on the right was 11th Panzer Division.

The strong Panther force was hampered by the fact that the tanks were brand new and their crews had had no chance of practising with them or ironing out any manufacturing defects. Two of the Panthers broke down before they even left the railway marshalling yards, and six more before they began their advance on 5 July. Mechanical breakdowns would continue to erode the number of Panthers in the front line throughout the battle.

In front of the XLVIII Panzer Corps were the Soviet 40th Army and 6th Guards Army. The units had been well dug in with all the ingenuity of which the Red Army was capable.

The advance ran into immediate trouble when a series of explosions brought a dozen Panthers to a grinding halt, their tracks blown off. The tanks had blundered into a Soviet minefield where no minefield was thought to exist. In all 36 Panthers were halted while sappers rushed forwards to try to clear the minefield and engineers sought to repair the broken tracks.

Before setting out on the offensive, the panzer crews had been given tactical directions on how to confront and overcome the Soviet defences. A critical part of these instructions read:

'In no circumstances will tanks be stopped to render assistance to those which have been disabled. Recovery is the responsibility of the engineer units only. Tank commanders are to press on to their objective as long as they retain mobility. Where a tank is rendered immobile but the gun is in working order (e.g. from mechanical failure or track damage) the crew will continue to give fire support from a static position.'

This instruction made sense in the invasion of France in

1940 and during 1941 and much of 1942, but by the end of 1942 the Soviet had adopted new defensive tactics, which were being put into practice on a large scale for the first time at Kursk. The Soviet anti-tank guns were put together in groups of between six and ten under a single commander who communicated with the guns by field telephone. This allowed the Soviets to fire all ten guns at a single target at the same time in co-ordination. The positioning of the guns meant that the target would be hit from several different directions at once. Given that panzers had very strong frontal armour, but weaker armour and vulnerable wheels on the flanks, this meant that whichever way a panzer faced at least some of the Soviet guns would be able to fire at a flank.

During earlier campaigns, the enemy anti-tank guns had been assaulted by infantry accompanying the panzers. These infantry were armed with light weaponry, backed by mortars and heavy machine-guns. But again the Soviets had learned the lessons of two years' fighting the Germans. Now the anti-tank batteries were protected by companies of infantry with their own machine-guns and mortars. These infantry were dug in and their positions camouflaged. They were under strict orders not to show themselves or open fire until the German infantry deployed to attack the guns they were defending. This ensured that the German infantry were taken by surprise and took casualties before they were able to eliminate the Soviet infantry and only then could they move on to tackle the anti-tank guns.

The upshot of these new Soviet tactics was that their anti-tank guns were more effective and survived longer than had previously been the case. Any tank that remained static for any length of time was therefore almost guaranteed to be targeted and reduced to a burning wreck. Orders to remain in a stationary tank and give covering fire to those still moving meant almost certain death for the panzer crew. And yet those were their orders.

Red Army infantry prepare to fire a PTRD anti-tank rifle from the shelter of a knocked-out tank at Kursk. Although effective in the early months of the war, the PTRD was useless against the new panzers fighting at Kursk.

As losses mounted among the panzers of XLVIII Panzer Corps, it was decided to send the infantry forwards to clear out the Soviet anti-tank guns. With the infantry went the handful of Tigers available, relying on their enormously strong armour to protect them as they used their 88 mm guns to destroy enemy positions. This was when the Soviet infantry showed themselves and opened fire. While they got short shrift from the Tigers, they seriously slowed down the German infantry.

At this point a small number of Il-2 ground-attack aircraft broke through the Luftwaffe fighter screen and came down to the attack. In reality the air attack was fairly light, certainly compared to what the Stukas routinely dished out to Soviet troops, but the Germans had become so accustomed to enjoying air supremacy that even this light attack came as a shock. It was a shock made all the worse by the fact that one bomb hit the command post of the Grossdeutschland Panzergrenadier Division and killed a number of senior officers.

Bogged down at the Berezovyy

By noon it was clear to Otto von Knobelsdorff, commanding XLVIII Panzer Corps, that things were going seriously awry. The OKH timetable said that he should by now have been through the first line of Red Army defences and starting to assault the second line. In fact most of his units had only just cleared the minefields and were starting to assault the defences of the first line.

Along much of his front, Knobelsdorff's men were – quite literally – getting bogged down. The Soviet first-line defences were around the villages of Butovo and Gertsovka. In front of the villages was the shallow dip that marked the valley of the Berezovyy stream. In itself the stream would not have been much of an obstacle. However, the Red Army engineers had dammed it some weeks earlier, causing the stream waters to flood out over the neighbouring meadows and thoroughly saturate them. When the Germans arrived, therefore, they were faced by a belt of muddy morass more than 200 m (650 ft) wide that would not support the weight of panzers and which gripped men's legs in a glutinous quagmire.

On the right flank of XLVIII Panzer Corps a group of Tigers, backed by Panzer IVs, found a way around the upper Berezovyy where the morass was narrower and less deep. By late afternoon they had blasted a gap through the Soviets' first line and were starting to move toward the second line. They paused while their officers studied the defences with field glasses, then called up Luftwaffe bombers to pound the more obvious strongpoints to dust.

To the right of Grossdeutschland Panzergrenadier Division, the lead units of 11th Panzer Division were also through the first line of defences and starting to get to grips with the minefields of the second line. By evening both units were starting to attack the Soviets' second line, with the Tigers leading the way. Elsewhere on the von Knobelsdorff front his men were still trying to clear the first line of defences.

The very success of the Tigers then began to be a problem. In places the Tigers had fought their way through Soviet defences, and rumbled on to take out more and more strongpoints. Their crews assumed that the Panzer III and Panzer IV support units were keeping up, when in fact they were not. The less well-armoured, older panzer models had taken much heavier casualties from Soviet anti-tank guns than had the Tigers, while the survivors were making only slow progress.

In places the Tigers were as much as 3.5 km (over 2 miles) ahead of any other German panzers. The gap had been cleared of Red Army men while the Tigers advanced, but now the empty ground was open to be taken by whoever could grab it. A savage battle erupted between German panzergrenadiers and Soviet infantry as both sought to flood into the land behind the Tigers.

The savage infantry fighting lasted long into the night, with heavy casualties on both sides. On the whole, the German infantry got the better of the fighting, though the willingness of the Soviets to feed in large numbers of reinforcements to replace men being killed did cause the fighting to be prolonged before the Germans secured the contested ground.

SS Panzer attack

To the right of von Knobelsdorff's XLVIII Panzer Corps the SS Panzer Corps of Paul Hausser faced the Soviet 6th Guards Army and 1st Tank Army. Hausser had at his disposal 42 Tigers plus 452 other tanks and self-propelled guns.

General Ivan Chistyakov, Commander of the 6th Guards Army, issued a declaration to his troops just before the battle in which he told them that the SS routinely shot all prisoners and wounded that fell into their hands. 'Comrades!' it continued. 'We face Hitler's guard. We must expect one of the main efforts of the German offensive in this sector.' Surrender was not an option and nor was retreat, so Chistyakov ordered his men to fight until they were killed.

As the elite troops they were, the SS troops had been well trained in assault tactics. As darkness fell on the night of 4 July, units of grenadiers crept forward to worm their way through the Soviet minefields and approach the front-line defences. When the German artillery bombardment began next morning, the SS grenadiers identified the key defensive positions. As soon as the bombardment lifted, the grenadiers dashed forwards to secure the defensive positions before the Red Army men could scramble out of their bunkers and bomb shelters to take up their posts. The SS therefore got a head start on their comrades.

The head start of the SS corps was maintained through a brutal combination of air support and determined action by the Tigers. With supporting infantry keeping pace with them to winkle out Soviet anti-tank defences, the Tigers and panzers pushed forward. At 9 am the SS men broke through the first line of defences near the village of Bykovka.

General Chistyakov was enjoying a breakfast of scrambled eggs and vodka with his staff when a Tiger lumbered into view and opened fire. Ignoring his own instructions to fight until killed, Chistyakov bolted rearwards until he reached the forward lines of the second defence line held by the 1st Guards Tank Army.

The SS Panzers were meanwhile finishing off Chistyakov's positions. A pause then came as the senior officers scanned the second line of defences and the towed artillery were brought up to deluge Soviet strongpoints.

At 3 pm a force of 42 Soviet T-34 tanks came racing out of cover to launch an attack on the SS Tigers. The fighting lasted more than two hours as the Soviets fed in more and more tanks to race around the panzers. By the time the T-34s retreated there were dozens of burning wrecks littering the fields, while the Germans had sustained only minor losses. It was not untypical for a Tiger tank to have half a dozen or more T-34s to its credit.

As the T-34s melted away the purpose of their near-suicidal assault became clear. While the tank fighting had been taking place the Soviet infantry had brought up additional anti-tank guns to bolster the section of line threatened by the SS panzers.

By early evening the Das Reich and Leibstandarte SS Adolf Hitler were confronting the Soviet second-line defences, though assaults delivered in the dying light were unsuccessful. However, the third SS division, the Totenkopf, had advanced barely half as far and had not yet got through the first Soviet line. In part this was due to the difficult marshy ground over which it was advancing, but also to the tenacious defence of the Soviet 52nd Guard Rifle Division, part of the 6th Guard Army.

When Hausser realized how far behind the Totenkopf had fallen, he called for help from General Hermann Breith, who commanded the III Panzer Corps to his right. Breith refused on the grounds that he was having trouble coping with his own problems.

Bridging the Donets

The main problem confronting Breith, and indeed all of Kempf's units, was that they had to get across the River Donets before they could get to grips with the Soviet defences. In theory this should not have been much of a problem. Kempf had been supplied with a large contingent of engineers to build bridges across the river. Painstaking work had gone into working out exactly where to place these bridges. Working from aerial photos, the German engineers prefabricated several bridges, each designed to be adequate to its allotted task – be it allowing Tigers, infantry or supply trucks to cross the river.

Unfortunately for the Germans, the Soviets had anticipated that such temporary bridges would be brought into play, and had even guessed where they might be positioned. As soon as it became clear that German sappers were clearing minefields, Soviet scouts pushed forward to locate exactly where the German bridges were being built. Those spots were heavily targeted by the Soviet pre-dawn bombardment. An indication of the difficulties the river caused can be gauged from the fact that of the entire 6th Panzer Division only a dozen Tigers and six battalions of infantry managed to get over the Donets by sunset that evening. Those units did move forwards, but quickly ran into a minefield that had not been properly cleared, as well as carefully camouflaged anti-tank guns. The attack came to a halt to await the rest of the division.

The 19th Panzer Division did a little better, but not much. They managed to get all their units over the river, but then found that the maps that they had been given by the army staff were incorrect and out of date. Nevertheless a determined offensive took the 19th Panzers some 8 km (5 miles) into Soviet territory by nightfall, and in places the first line of defences had been breached.

To the right of the 19th Panzer Division, the 7th Panzer Division hit a problem that had nothing to do with the Soviets. Nobody had told the engineers that the 7th Panzers included Tigers, so the bridges thrown over the Donets had been designed to take only Panzer IIIs and Panzer IVs. They would have simply collapsed if a Tiger had tried to cross.

After some frantic work a ford was found and the Tigers drove there only to find that the far bank was too marshy for the heavy tanks to use. The engineers had meanwhile been bringing up additional materials and by 3 pm had managed to strengthen one bridge enough to cope with Tigers. The impatient panzer crews drove straight across and into action.

The rest of the 7th Panzers were pinned down by dense Soviet anti-tank defences. The arrival of the Tigers transformed the situation. Using their established move-stop-aim-fire-move-stop-aim-fire tactics, the Tigers swiftly punched through the first line of Soviet defences, then rumbled on towards the second line – while the older panzers and infantry proceeded to clear out the surviving Soviet soldiers. By dusk the Tigers were 10 km (over 6 miles) into Soviet territory, but had not managed to punch through the second line of defences as the German plan called for.

To the right of the 7th Panzers, Raus and his two infantry divisions had also crossed the river and they fell on the defenders. The Soviets were taken by surprise by the swift advance of the German infantry and fell back in confusion. As the element of surprise was lost the Soviet resistance became tougher and in mid afternoon about 40 T-34 tanks came forward in a counter-attack. Raus had brought forward anti-tank guns for just such an event, but the scale and speed of the Soviet tank advance was unexpected and took time to defeat. By nightfall, Raus's men were 3.5 km (2 miles) into the Soviet defences and had in places got through the first line of defences. They had, however, taken heavier than expected casualties and Raus was wary of his chances of success.

Walter Model (1891–1945)

Model was the son of a music teacher with no military connections. Nevertheless he joined the army in 1908 and enjoyed an unspectacular career until he was badly wounded in 1915. Returning to duty, he was posted to the general staff, where he proved to be highly talented at military administration, though he was found to have a habit of speaking bluntly to his superiors. After the war he remained in the army, writing military biographies in his spare time.

He began the war on the staff, but was soon given command of the 3rd Panzer Division. There he began an unconventional training programme that made his division one of the finest in the German army. He served under Guderian in the invasion of Russia, fighting a series of fast-moving panzer actions that ended in sweeping victories. During the Soviet counter-attacks over the winter of 1941–2 he conducted several brilliant defensive battles. After one meeting during this period, Hitler remarked, 'I trust that man, but I would not want to serve under him.'

After Kursk, Model was relieved of his command of the 9th Army, but three months later he was sent to take over Army Group North, where he ended a Soviet offensive. In August 1944 he was transferred to Normandy with orders to stop the Allied invasion of France. He succeeded in slowing the Allies, but could not stop them. He defeated the Allied attack on Arnhem and then designed tough defences. Instead of his favoured strategy of flexible defence and counter-attack, Hitler ordered Model to launch the massive offensive that became known as the Battle of the Bulge. After the defeat of that move, Model reverted to the defence.

On 15 April, Model discharged all the men under his command from the army and told them to choose whether to surrender or seek to fight on. He himself walked off to attack the Americans. His body was found on 21 April, and it is usually thought that he committed suicide rather than surrender.

Colonel General Otto Moritz Walter Model on a command post near Oryol, Russia in July, 1943.

Reinforcing the Soviet line

By the close of the first day of fighting it was already clear
that the German plan was not working. Nowhere had the
Germans breached the second line of Soviet defences, while
the plans drawn up at OKH had confidently predicted that
this line would have crumbled completely by nightfall.

That failure was not only disappointing in itself, but also
fraught with danger. The Soviets now knew exactly the
planned lines of advance being taken by the major German
advances. They could afford to move units away from less
threatened sectors and use them to bolster the areas of the
front being subjected to attack. Such a movement would take
time. If the Germans had been through the second line of
defences on the first day, they would almost certainly have
been able to power forwards fast enough to be through the
Soviet defences entirely before the reinforcements could
come up. Now, however, the Soviets would have time to get
their reinforcements into position in time to face the
Germans head-on.

The reinforcements the Soviets were bringing up were
strong. In the south six new infantry divisions and no less
than 1,000 tanks were on their way. In the north two infantry
corps and 600 tanks came forwards to face the central section
of the German attack.

Taking stock: progress so far

From the German point of view the first day of the battle had
not gone as well as expected, but neither had it been especially
disappointing. They had hoped to break through the second

line of defences in the afternoon, but had not done so. Nevertheless the first line of defences had been overcome and in places the Germans were penetrating into the second line of defences.

For the Soviets, likewise, things had not gone entirely to plan, but neither were they disastrous. The first line of defences had given way quicker than expected, but the German offensive had so far been contained. No breakthrough had been achieved, and reinforcements were being brought up to strengthen threatened areas.

What was clear to everyone was that this was already a very different style of battle to anything seen before on the Eastern Front. Carefully prepared defences were being ground down by equally carefully prepared offensives – though at the cost of casualties much higher than the Germans were accustomed to accepting. There was no sign of the sweeping manoeuvres and thrusting panzer columns of the previous two years. Kursk was a static battle of attrition that was quite alien to the German way of waging war.

While the senior staff on both sides of the conflict studied reports, located units on maps and tried to make sense of what was going on, the skies over Kursk erupted into a thunderstorm of epic proportions. It did not last long, but it was to have a dramatic effect on the next day's fighting.

Chapter 7

BREAKTHROUGH

By sunset on 5 July 1943 General Model, who was commanding the German attacks on the northern flank of the Kursk salient, believed that he had identified the keys to victory. If he could only grab them, he would be in a position to smash the Soviet defenders he faced.

Blocking the German advance on the left centre of Model's front was the village of Ponyri, which had been heavily fortified by the Red Army. Meanwhile the right centre of the front was overlooked by the hills around Olkhovatka, from which Soviet artillery could pound advancing German units. By taking those two positions, Model would be able to unlock the second line of Soviet defences. The road to Kursk would be open. Consequently, Model's staff spent the night issuing orders to regroup the attack forces to redirect their energies against Ponyri and Olkhovatka.

Surprise onslaught

But just before dawn it was the Soviets who attacked, not the Germans. Rokossovsky had identified the German advance toward Olkhovatka as the most dangerous part of the front. He ordered the 2nd Tank Army, supported by two infantry corps and other units, to attack the nose of the German advance and push it back away from Olkhovatka. This counter-attack was to be supported by the Soviet air force.

The Soviet airmen had learnt from their defeats the previous day. Instead of attempting to win air superiority, still less air supremacy, over the battlefield they sought to achieve a purely local and temporary command of the air. Rokossovsky's 16th Air Army was commanded by Sergei Rudenko, a cobbler's son who had joined the Red Army in 1923 and then been ordered into the air force three years later when nobody volunteered. In the early months of the war, Rudenko commanded the 31st Air Division, where he presided over massive losses to the technologically superior German aircraft and better-trained German aircrew. Gradually the Soviet air force became better trained and better equipped, and Rudenko improved his skills as well. He took command of the 16th Air Army in October 1942 and worked tirelessly to improve its combat effectiveness.

Now, on the second day of the Kursk battle, Rudenko took the brave decision to ignore his orders – a dangerous thing to do when Stalin was constantly demanding to know if the Soviets had achieved control of the air. Rudenko decided to allow the Germans undisputed air supremacy over those areas that he considered to be of secondary importance. He would withdraw his aircraft from those areas so that he could concentrate his entire force over the small parts of the battlefield that he thought were crucially important.

As the sun came up on 6 July the area of greatest importance was the low land north of Olkhovatka. Rudenko sent in massed squadrons of bombers and ground-attack aircraft to pound the German positions, while clouds of fighters circled overhead to keep the German aircraft occupied. The tactic succeeded, giving the Soviets temporary control over a relatively small area and allowing the bombers to operate without interference from the Luftwaffe.

It proved to be a disappointment to Rudendko that his change of tactics and valour of his airmen ended up being wasted. Due to a breakdown in the Soviet communications systems, most of the units supposed to be taking part in the dawn counter-offensive did not get their orders until mid morning. The only unit that got moving on time was the 16th Tank Corps of the 2nd Tank Army. Equipped with 200 tanks, mostly T-34s but with a few heavier KV-1 tanks, the 16th Tank Corps came racing out of the dawn gloom toward the nose of the German advance. It was sheer bad luck for the Soviets that they ran headlong into the 26 Tigers of the 505th Heavy Tank Battalion of XLVII Panzer Corps. Within less than an hour 69 Soviet tanks were flaming wrecks and the rest were retreating. The Germans had not lost a single tank, although two Tigers were slightly damaged and were taken to the rear for repair.

Model makes his move

The Soviet attack had ended in failure, but it had caused Model to delay the start of his own attack for two hours. That attack was preceded by a short, heavy artillery bombardment and accompanied by intense air attacks. Model had also brought up some of the units he had been holding in reserve. He had told his commanders that he expected to break through Soviet defences this day and so had his main fighting force ready to erupt through the gap.

Ponyri was attacked by the 9th Panzer Division while the 2nd Panzer Division spearheaded the attack toward Olkhovatka; both units were supported by infantry divisions that had been in action the previous day. The Soviet artillery and anti-tank fire was even heavier than it had been the day before and German losses rose accordingly. The fighting was murderous and increasingly static. As quickly as Soviet defenders were killed, they were replaced – so that no matter what losses the Germans inflicted they could make no headway. To add variety to the horror, the Soviets launched a series of armoured attacks. At 6.30 pm the largest of these saw 150 tanks of 19th Tank Corps charge at the 2nd Panzer Division. The Soviets were driven off with heavy losses, but the Germans were no further forwards.

Struggle for Ponyri – and 'Hill 253.5'

The most intense fighting proved to be at Ponyri. The village was a long, straggling affair that had begun as a typical farming village but had grown after a railway station was built nearby. Over the years the village had spread out to embrace the station. Although most villages in the area were made of wood or turf, Ponyri had substantial brick buildings, especially near the station where there were warehouses, silos and more modern workers' housing.

The attack began at dawn with a heavy raid by German bombers and Stukas that blasted the Soviet defences to pieces.

These defences proved, however, to have been only the most forward works in a dense network of defensive positions that filled the entire village and the fields around it. As the German infantry and tanks pushed forwards, they soon discovered that the path cleared for them by the bombers was only a path through to further Soviet defences. By lunchtime the Germans had captured more than half of Ponyri, but then a Soviet counter-attack was launched that drove them back. The Germans tried again, and again had nearly captured the village when large Soviet reinforcements arrived and drove them back.

Meanwhile another German attack had been launched 8 km (5 miles) to the east. The Germans were aiming for a patch of high ground that they codenamed 'Hill 253.5'. Taking the hill would allow them to site artillery so that it could rain shells down on Soviet positions in Ponyri and blast any trucks bringing up supplies to the defenders.

The attack over open country began with a combined infantry-panzer thrust, but this was not pushed with any vigour. The move had been designed to make the Soviet defenders, in particular the anti-tank guns, open fire and so reveal their positions. Then came the Stukas, which dived from the skies to release their bombs with pinpoint accuracy to smash the Soviet bunkers and gun emplacements. With those positions destroyed and Red Army soldiers dead or fleeing, the panzers and infantry advanced again. When they were again forced to stop they once more called up air support. It was a gruelling and vicious advance with heavy casualties on both sides. By dusk Hill 253.5 was still in Soviet hands.

Appraisal – and a new plan

As dusk fell on 6 July, Model held an appraisal meeting at his headquarters. The German losses in the first two days of the offensive had been heavier than expected and no breakthrough had been achieved. However, the Soviet losses had been staggering and their forces had been pushed back several kilometres.

Model deduced that the Soviet defences must be close to collapse and so decided on a renewed assault next day with some of his reserves being released to strengthen the attack. But he was underestimating the willingness of Soviet commanders to accept huge losses, and of the Red Army men to march into positions where they knew they stood little chance of survival.

Model decided that the main targets for his attacks on 7 July, as on the 6 July, would be Ponyri and the Olkhovatka hills, but with the village of Teploe to the west of Olkhovatka included. A victory at Teploe would allow the panzers to race across open country to cut off the defenders of Olkhovatka from their supplies. This time the panzer divisions would take the lead. The 9th Panzers were to attack Ponyri, the 2nd Panzers would tackle Olkhovatka and the 20th Panzers would head for Teploe.

A refinement to Model's plan of attack came in the form of 500 aircraft that von Richthofen had agreed to send from the southern face of the salient to support this attack. The extra aircraft were available only for a single attack just after dawn, but Model was determined to make the most of it. The Luftwaffe pummelled the Soviet defences, opening a route for the panzers. Once again, however, the apparently cleared path led only to more Soviet defences. The depth of the defended zone appeared endless to the tiring German troops.

Nevertheless, the Germans were making progress. At 11 am the 2nd Panzer Division got through the Soviet second-line defences for the first time. Turning to the sides, the panzers, self-propelled guns and infantry began assaulting neighbouring Soviet units in flank and rear. By noon a 3-km (nearly 2-mile) gap had been created in the Soviet defences. Model diverted the 20th Panzer Division from its attack on Teploe to take advantage of the breakthrough. Together with elements of the 2nd Panzer Division, the 20th drove through the gap and headed for the Olkhovatka hills.

The Soviets had had some warning that their crumbling defences were about to collapse. Rudenko had therefore been hoarding his aircraft to mount another of his massive but limited strikes. A vast cloud of Soviet aircraft struck at the narrow 3-km (2-mile) gap, firing at anything that moved. The Luftwaffe fighter screen was overwhelmed by the sudden onslaught. The German dislocation was only temporary as aerial reinforcements were soon brought up, but it did give Rudenko's ground-attack aircraft precious minutes in which to attack the German panzers and motorized infantry vehicles.

No sooner had the Soviet aircraft gone than more than 60 T-34s loomed out of the smoke. Another fast-moving tank battle developed, with the Soviet vehicles constantly on the move seeking to get around the rear of the panzers, while the panzer commanders co-operated in destroying Soviet armour and fending off their attacks.

The tank attack was eventually driven off with heavy losses, but the swirling combat had seriously disordered the German panzers and dislocated their links to the infantry that were supposed to be supporting them. By the time everything had been sorted out dusk was gathering and the chance to launch a surprise attack on the Olkhovatka hills had been lost.

The attack on Ponyri also proved to be a murderous assault with limited gains. The Soviets had brought up several new artillery batteries during the night and dug them in to carefully camouflaged positions. The 9th Panzer Division with its supporting infantry made continual advances, but at a very slow rate and at the cost of casualties. By nightfall about 80 per cent of the town was firmly in German hands.

Model considered that his gains had been steady if unspectacular. Again Soviet losses had been huge, and although his own had been heavy they were not insupportable. The attack, he decided, would go on. The 4th Panzer Division was brought out of reserve to support the attack on Olkhovatka.

Dogged Soviet resilience

Rokossovsky also recognized the huge losses that his forces had been suffering, but was prepared to accept them. He decided to take a risk on the night of 7 July by moving the IX Tank Corps up to the front line. This corps had been earmarked to fight a rearguard action should the Germans break through the Soviet defences. Their task would be to hold up the German advance to allow the Soviet forces to evacuate the Kursk salient and so escape being surrounded and annihilated. By committing them to battle, Rokossovsky was making this an all-or-nothing struggle. Either he would win, or be utterly defeated.

The next day dawned dull and wet. Low cloud stopped air activity, which hampered the Germans more than the Soviets. The air conditions improved by mid morning and the Luftwaffe took to the skies, but by then the ground attack had already begun.

At 9 am a new gap opened up in the Soviet defence line in front of Teploe. The fresh 4th Panzer Division and 2nd Panzer Division surged through. The 2nd Panzers headed for Olkhovatka, while the 4th drove for Teploe. The 4th Panzers were met by heavy fire, but drove on and smashed through the defences around the village. The panzers then swung southeast to attack the Olkhovatka hills from the west as the 2nd Panzers attacked from the north. One Soviet position after another was destroyed and overrun, but always there was another anti-tank gun or infantry-filled trench to be faced. By nightfall the panzers were halfway up the slopes of the hills, but not yet on the high ground.

At Ponyri the Germans had achieved much less. Soviet counter-attacks pushed them back to the centre of the village. Both sides brought up reinforcements, which only served to keep the opposing forces equal. The fighting lurched back and forth but, despite the shedding of huge quantities of blood, the rival forces ended the day only a few yards from where they had begun.

By the end of 8 July the senior officers of von Greim's 6th Air Fleet were beginning to notice a problem. Their units were starting to run short of lubricants, oil and other key essential supplies. As aircraft reached the point at which their engines or guns needed servicing they were having to be withdrawn from action for longer and longer periods of time. Thus, without suffering particularly heavy combat losses, the Luftwaffe was finding itself with fewer and fewer aircraft available for missions.

The root of the problem lay in the usual meticulous staff work of OKH. They had anticipated that the ground troops would break through the Soviet defences on day two of the campaign. Thereafter the panzers would surge at speed across the Russian steppe to reach Kursk, with motorized infantry following at speed to seal off the neck of the salient and trap the huge number of Soviet soldiers so that they could be captured or killed with relative ease.

Priority over supply trucks and trains running during the attack itself had therefore been given to the panzer and panzer-grenadier divisions. The Luftwaffe was expected to use up the stockpiles that had been built up before the offensive began. Those were considered to be adequate for the first three or four days of fighting, after which the Luftwaffe was expected to be undertaking fewer missions.

In fact, the expected breakthrough on the ground had not taken place, so Luftwaffe demands were as great as ever. Inevitably the Luftwaffe was not able to keep up with calls for ground attacks being received from ground units. Even more concerning was the fact that German fighters were no longer able to patrol the skies over the battlefield in numbers large enough to retain control of the air. Slowly but surely the unde-feated Luftwaffe was losing the air campaign to the increasingly battered Soviet air force simply because of the supply situation.

The next day, 9 July, Model summoned Harpe and Lemelson,

commanders of XLI and XLVII Panzer Corps respectively, to a conference that was also attended by von Kluge, commander of the entire Army Group Centre. Studying battle reports and the latest updates, the four senior officers concluded that the 9th Army was highly unlikely to achieve a breakthrough. The Soviet defences, as Model had long feared, were simply too tough to be broken by a frontal assault.

Although the German officers at the impromptu conference on 9 July recognized that they were beaten, von Kluge insisted that the offensive had to continue. If it did not, then the Soviets would be able to transfer units from the northern face of the salient to the southern to face Manstein's attack. After this conference, the 9th Army continued its attacks on Olkhovatka and on Ponyri, but the assaults were never again on a major scale. Increasingly attacks were designed to provoke a Soviet counter-attack in which the Red Army units would emerge into the open where they could more easily be destroyed.

Southern flank

While Model and Rokossovky were fighting each other to a bloody stalemate in the north, Manstein and Vatutin were also slogging it out on the southern flank of the Kursk salient.

After dark on 5 July, the first day of the offensive, Vatutin had been sent the 1 Tank Army. He and Zhukov debated whether to use it to launch a counter-attack or to put it into the second line of defences to bolster them. In the end they went for the latter. Many of the tanks were dug into emplacements so that only their turrets showed above ground. They were thus being used as artillery, not as tanks.

On Hoth's left the XLVIII Panzer Corps of Otto von Knobelsdorff began 6 July by finishing their task of breaking through the first line of Soviet defences. They then drove north expecting to find a second line of defences, but instead encountering the River Pena. After the previous night's thunderstorm the Pena was in flood, with a wide belt of meadows reduced to swamp that could not be crossed by the heavy panzers.

Knobelsdorff ordered his panzers to veer to the east to work their way around the shallower upper reaches of the Pena. This brought them closer to the left flank of the SS Panzer Corps to their right, which considerably narrowed the front on which the Germans were advancing – causing some congestion among the supply trucks bringing up the rear.

Once past the Pena, the XLVIII Panzer Corps ran into the Soviet second defence line. After a quick appraisal, the attack began. As before, the Soviet positions were fronted by large minefields and tank-proof ditches that forced the panzers either to halt or to travel along routes where the Soviet gunners had their range. Behind these obstacles were the usual networks of anti-tank guns and infantry trenches. The defences were strengthened by the dug-in tanks that had arrived the night before.

The Germans had been expecting to encounter the second line of defences, but had not expected it to be as strong as it was. Knobelsdorff soon realized that he would not be able to get through the lines on 6 July, even though his initial plans had called for him to smash past them on 5 July. In fact the Grossdeutschland Division did manage to pierce a small gap late in the evening, but were unable to expand or exploit it before night fell.

SS commander Paul Hausser was instrumental in forming the Waffen-SS to fight in the front line alongside the regular army and at Kursk commanded the II SS Panzer Corps.

SS panzers break through

Meanwhile, to Knobelsdorff's right in the centre of Manstein's attack, the II SS Panzer Corps of Paul Hausser began an attack a short time before dawn. The assault was preceded by a heavy artillery barrage, then – as the sun came up – raids by Luftwaffe bombers. Directly in front of the SS corps was the village of Pokrovka, the centre for several road junctions. One of those roads led north-east to Prokhorovka, which straddled the key railway line from Moscow to Kharkov by way of Kursk. Hausser's task for the day was to capture Pokrovka and mass for an assault up the road towards the railway line.

The SS attack began well, as it had the previous day. The Tigers went in first to blast Soviet strongpoints and destroy anti-tank guns with their fearsome 88 mm gun while being protected by their tough armour. Behind the Tigers came Panzer IVs and panzergrenadiers. By 10 am the Tigers were through the second line of Soviet defences. After a short pause while the gap was widened and secured, the panzers began the drive north through open country.

The SS panzer commanders were soon to discover that the landscape was not as empty as it seemed. While there was no continuous belt of Soviet defences, there were strongpoints, some of them very strong indeed. These were located in fortified villages or the small hills that rose from otherwise flat plains. Each strongpoint was ringed by mines, equipped with anti-tank guns and seething with infantry. Each strongpoint took time to destroy, slowing down the advance of the SS panzers.

Pokrovka was captured soon after noon, though not without intense house-to-house fighting by the infantry. The panzers, meanwhile, swept on through the more open country to the east of Pokrovka. They were now well into the Soviet rear areas and coming up against some unexpected opponents.

One group of Tigers from the Leibstandarte SS Adolf Hitler Division found itself faced by two batteries of massively powerful 152 mm artillery. These heavy guns had a range of almost 16 km (10 miles) and fired a shell that weighed more than 40 kg (880 lb). The Tigers were commanded by Michael Wittmann, one of the most talented panzer commanders of the war. Moving through dead ground and woodlands, Wittmann eventually got close enough to the Soviet guns to be able to open fire. Wittmann had all five Tigers fire at once, a salvo that smashed the first Soviet battery and began a fire that a few minutes later caused the Soviet ammunition to explode. The Tigers then raced on to destroy the second battery before the Soviet gunners could aim at the panzers. It was a minor victory, though one that enhanced Wittmann's reputation. Once again, however, the Germans had been slowed down.

By nightfall Hausser had achieved his allotted tasks. However, he and his men were painfully aware that the units on their flanks had not kept up as they were supposed to have done. That left the flanks of the SS divisions dangerously exposed to Soviet counter-attacks. Hausser had to divert nearly one-third of his tanks away from the offensive head of his units to defensive positions along their flanks.

It was Hausser's right flank that was most exposed, a fact caused by the inability of Army Detachment Kempf to advance as far or as fast as it should have done. Kempf's panzer divisions had moved forwards at dawn, like the SS accompanied by artillery and Luftwaffe attacks. They found themselves moving into a complex web of minefields and anti-tank guns that took time and effort to break through. Soon after noon the Soviets launched a series of localized counter-attacks that served to slow down whatever advances the Germans were making and to disrupt their communications. By the time night fell Kempf was not very much further forwards and had still not reached, never mind broken through, the second line of Soviet defences.

As night fell on the second day of battle, Hoth knew that he was making good progress against determined opposition, but was behind schedule. Rather more alarming was the number of Tiger and Panther tanks that were being forced to leave the battle due to engine breakdowns and other mechanical problems. These were the secret weapons that had been supposed to guarantee victory, and yet here they were being lost to Hoth even though the Soviets had found no answer to their formidable fighting power.

Strengthening defences

If Hoth was facing up to the fact that things were not going as well as they could have done, so was Vatutin. By the evening of 6 July he had thrown nearly all his reserves into the battle and yet there was no sign of any slackening in the German advance. At 6.30 pm Vatutin sent a message to the Stavka giving a detailed assessment of the situation and stating that unless he received substantial reinforcements within 48 hours the Germans would break through.

Stalin read Vatutin's report at a meeting of the Stavka.

Within minutes the decision had been taken to send Vatutin two tank corps from the South-western Front that neighboured Vatutin's Voronezh Front to the south. Those units would arrive within the stipulated 48 hours. Also being sent to aid Vatutin was to be the entire 5th Guards Tank Army, which composed well over one-third of Konev's Steppe Front.

When he received orders to detach the 5th Guards Tank Army and send it to Vatutin, Konev was not unnaturally annoyed. Not only was he being asked to lose one-third of his army, but the unit contained nearly all his armoured vehicles. Konev pointed out that the task of his unit was to attack with overwhelming strength any German breakthrough, not to detach units piecemeal to shore up crumbling defences. Stalin phoned Konev and a fairly heated discussion of military strategy followed, which ended with Stalin telling Konev bluntly to obey his orders.

The 5th Guards Tank Army was on the move the following morning. Its commander, Alexei Zhadov, estimated he would enter Vatutin's command area at Prokhorovka on 11 July.

On 7 July some 500 aircraft from von Richthofen's air fleet went north to assist Model's offensive, so there was less in the way of air support for Manstein's forces. Despite this the German ground forces continued their offensive. The dawn brought a fog along much of the front, which served to mask the German movements from Soviet gunners until the last moment.

Knobelsdorff's XLVIII Panzer Corps began the day by seeking to exploit the small gap in the Soviet second-line defences made by the Grossdeutschland Division late the previous day. At 6 am the Panthers went forward, but almost at once ran into a minefield planted by the Soviets overnight and came to a halt. Once the mines were cleared the panzers got on the move again and by noon had widened the gap in the Soviet defences.

As the panzers pushed through the gap they were met by a sudden counter-attack launched by 100 T-34 tanks, again adopting the new tactics of swarming forwards at high speed. As before, the Soviet attack was driven off with heavy losses, but not before the Germans had been delayed. Undeterred, the panzers now turned west to take Soviet defenders in flank and rear. This move continued until the Germans had reached the positions that they would have occupied if they had been able to advance directly north over the Pena the day before.

That night the Soviet engineers went out to lay more minefields, only to be met by strong detachments of German infantry guarding the German engineers who were coming forward to clear the same mines. A savage firefight broke out in the darkness that lasted almost until dawn.

The main effort of the II SS Panzer Corps on Knobelsdorff's right flank, meanwhile, went into their own exposed right flank as they sought to link up with the struggling Army Detachment Kempf. It was hoped that a quick advance through the village of Teterevino would bring the SS panzers on to the rear of the Soviet III Tank Corps that had been holding the two German corps apart and force them to retreat. Any hope that the Soviet defences would be facing south and could be taken in flank were quickly dispelled. The assault soon became as costly and slow as any other.

Heroics of Corporal Franz Staudegger

The most celebrated event of the day came near the village of Psyolknee when 50 T-34 tanks swarmed forwards in an effort to blunt the attack of the Leibstandarte SS Adolf Hitler Division. Positioned a distance ahead of the other panzers was a lone Tiger commanded by Corporal Franz Staudegger. Realizing that the Soviet tank commanders had not seen his tank, Staudegger decided to allow them to move forwards before launching an attack into the flank of the Soviet formation. In the 40 minutes that followed, Staudegger destroyed no less than 40 Soviet tanks, and gave up shooting only because he ran out of ammunition and the Soviets were in retreat.

After Staudegger's extraordinary claim was verified by counting the burning T-34 wrecks, he was promoted to sergeant and recommended for the Knight's Cross of the Iron Cross, the highest award for battlefield bravery in the German Army. A few days later Staudegger was flown to meet Hitler at OKH headquarters so that he could retell the story of the battle in person.

By 7 pm the village of Teterevino had fallen and the SS units pushed on east. As hoped, this did cause the Soviet forces further south to pull back to avoid being surrounded, but they moved slowly and fought all the way.

Army Detachment Kempf, meanwhile, was still advancing only slowly northwards. It began to make real progress only after the SS corps had captured Teterevino and by then it was so late in the day that little could be achieved before nightfall. Determined not to leave his SS comrades in the lurch with an open flank, Kempf ordered a nocturnal attack to take place at just past midnight in the hope that this would take the Soviets by surprise.

The move did indeed surprise them and allowed Kempf's units to make progress, but Mikhail Shumilov, who commanded the 7th Guards Army in front of Kempf, was determined to keep the Germans tied down. No sooner had he heard of the German attack than he threw his reserves into a counter-attack and the night fighting fizzled out in a bloody stalemate.

At Soviet HQ

That night of 7 July two things took place at Vatutin's headquarters that are worth remark. The first was that Stalin's personal envoy to Vatutin called the staff officers together and made a speech. This was Nikita Khrushchev, the man who would take over as Soviet leader after Stalin's death. As part of his political haranguing of the military officers, Khrushchev declared, 'The next two or three days will be terrible. Either we hold out or the Germans take Kursk. They are staking everything on this one card. It is a matter of life or death. We must make sure that we break their necks.' Quite what the officers made of this political tub-thumping is not recorded.

The other event at Vatutin's headquarters was the despatch to the Stavka of an up-to-date report on the situation, along with a detailed breakdown of estimated German losses. The original of this report has been lost, but the Stavka authorized the public release of what they claimed were its contents. According to this version, the German panzers had been suffering immense losses. On the first day of the attack, the Soviets claimed, the Germans had lost 250 Tiger tanks and 769 other tanks. During the following two days of fighting another 70 Tigers and 450 other tanks had been destroyed. In all, the Soviets were claiming, the Germans had lost 320 Tigers and 1,219 other tanks.

Given that the Germans had deployed less than 3,000 tanks in all the claims were clearly ridiculously wrong. Debate has raged ever since as to whether the claim was entirely fictitious and dreamed up in Moscow by some propaganda staff to try to boost morale, or whether the Soviet Army really thought it was inflicting this sort of damage on the Germans.

Whatever the truth, Vatutin clearly knew he was in trouble. He ordered the 40th Army to move from its position west of the German advance to start attacking the flanks of the XLVIII Panzer Corps in an effort to slow down the advance of that unit.

The fighting on 8 July was largely taken up with Vatutin's counter-attack. As with other Soviet counter-attacks improvised during the fighting around Kursk, the offensive failed to achieve much. Bad communications and faulty planning resulted in the Soviet units moving up in unco-ordinated fashion so that they could be picked off one by one by the Germans. One unforeseen result of Kempf's abortive night assault of the night before came on 8 July. The Tigers of 503rd Battalion that led the 6th Panzer Division broke through the Soviet second defensive line in the morning and drove northeast encountering almost no opposition. The other panzers followed and by nightfall they had penetrated 16 km (10 miles) beyond the Soviet defences, but had managed to open up a corridor only 3.5 km (2 miles) wide. Such an extended finger was highly vulnerable to a flank attack. The rest of Kempf's force continued its agonizingly slow advance.

The following day the German advance began again. The Grossdeutschland Division finally smashed through the last Soviet defences at the village of Gremutshy. That afternoon the SS raced across open country, turning west to attack Soviet positions from the rear and open up the way for the rest of the II SS Panzer Corps and the XLVIII Panzer Corps to their left.

That night Hoth talked with Manstein. They decided that the two corps were to spend the following day opening and expanding the breach in the Soviet lines with infantry and artillery while the panzers were given a day to repair their tanks, re-equip and reorganize ready for the final thrust towards Kursk.

The stage was set for the greatest tank battle in history.

Chapter 8

THE GREAT TANK BATTLE

When night fell on 11 July the commanders on both sides knew that the crisis point in the Battle of Kursk had been reached. In the north Model's German 9th Army had given up all hope of breaking through the tough Soviet defences. Instead, Model was launching a series of limited offensives designed to tie up Soviet forces and inflict casualties.

It was in the south where Manstein's Army Group South was still making progress that the fate of the offensive was going to be decided. The Germans had spent the previous day preparing to launch a major tank advance into the open country beyond the main Soviet defensive works, through which they had finally fought their way.

Thus far in the battle, the Germans had been fighting their way directly north as if heading straight for the city of Kursk. However, astride their route were some forested hills that were unsuitable for panzer fighting, so Hoth and Manstein had already decided that once through the Soviet defences they would turn east toward the small town of Prokhorovka before veering north again. This would allow them to advance across relatively flat, open farmland ideal for tank warfare.

A Soviet photo that purports to show a Soviet soldier inspecting German Panzer III tanks destroyed at Prokhorovka. In fact, Germany lost only one Panzer III that day, so the photo must show some other incident.

German orders

Late in the evening of 11 July the German orders for the next day's fighting were issued. The II SS Panzer Corps led by Paul Hausser was to lead the attack north-east to Prokhorovka, while other units advanced on their flanks seeking to widen and exploit the gap smashed by the Waffen-SS.

Hausser deployed his three divisions with Totenkopf on the left, Leibstandarte in the centre and Das Reich on the right. His plan was for Leibstandarte and Das Reich to open the attack at dawn by advancing as if intending to attack the main Soviet defences in front of Prokhorovka. This was merely a ruse to keep the Soviet troops pinned down. The Totenkopf was meanwhile to race through relatively thinly defended country to the north-west of Prokhorovka along the valley of the River Psel. Having got on to the flank of the Soviets defending Prokhorovka, Totenkopf was to turn sharply south-east and take them from the rear. Combined with a renewed assault by Leibstandarte this would destroy the Soviet defences. Das Reich would then swoop to the south of Prokhorovka to race on and open up the entire Soviet rear areas in classic *blitzkrieg* fashion. Thereafter the whole of Hoth's 4th Panzer Army would be able to attack and roll up the Soviet lines.

To undertake this task, Hausser had only 294 tanks and assault guns, of which 15 were Tigers. After a full week of fighting, many of his armoured vehicles had either been knocked out or broken down.

The Germans had been expecting the Soviets to deploy reinforcements brought up from the rear to stop a breakthrough.

Over the previous two days Soviet counter-offensives had been taking place, but had been beaten off. Hoth assumed that these were the expected Soviet reserves, not realizing that they had actually been units brought up from other areas of the front. The real Soviet reserves were in fact mustering near Prokhorovka, ready to launch a surprise offensive of their own.

Soviet counter-assault

The Soviet forces gathering to face the II SS Panzer Corps were massive. They consisted of the 5th Guards Army and 5th Guards Tank Army. The 5th Guards Army under Alexei Zhadov was largely an infantry force, with seven infantry divisions plus the 10th Tank Corps, a relatively weak unit comprising three tank brigades and one brigade of motorized infantry.

The 5th Guards Tank Army was a considerably stronger force consisting of three tank corps and two mechanized infantry corps. It could muster 850 tanks, plus numerous other vehicles and guns.

The commander of the 5th Guards Tank Army, Pavel Rotmistrov, had command of the entire operation. On the evening of 11 July, Vatutin ordered that all units of his Voronezh Front were to launch attacks the next morning. To Rotmistrov he gave specific orders that he was to attack and destroy the three SS divisions of the II SS Panzer Corps. In particular, he was to use his numerically superior forces to surround the Germans and deny them the chance to escape by retreating.

Having barely received Vatutin's orders and begun to draw up his plan, Rotmistrov received news that the German III

Panzer Corps of Army Detachment Kempf had launched a surprise evening assault and had captured Rzhavets. This assault was one of the most dramatic incidents in the entire campaign.

'Soviet' advance takes Germans beyond enemy lines

The Germans had got hold of a T-34 with a still-functioning engine. They then painted several other tanks and half-tracks to resemble Soviet vehicles and improved the deception with wooden guns and bulges to alter the silhouettes of the vehicles. The panzergrenadiers were told to sit on the tanks, as Soviet infantry did, and to lounge about as if relaxing and smoking cigarettes. To increase the illusion the men were encouraged to laugh and wave. On no account, however, was anyone to say a single word.

The column then moved forward after dark to approach the forward Soviet positions as if they were an advance patrol falling back after a hard day's fighting. The men in the first Soviet positions called out and waved, the Germans waved back and passed on. Once into Soviet-held territory the going was rather easier as the Soviet troops they passed clearly did not expect Germans to be in the area.

As the column reached the outskirts of Rzhavets a column of 20 T-34 tanks rumbled past going the other way. The sixth Soviet tank from the rear came to an abrupt stop. The tank commander peered at the passing panzers, then shouted a warning and began traversing his turret. The Germans reacted faster and opened fire, destroying the T-34. The remarkable journey was over and the fight was on.

The panzers and panzergrenadiers attacked the Soviet defences from the rear while the main force launched a frontal assault. By dawn the Germans were in Rzhavets and had secured a bridgehead over the Donets. Reinforcements were pouring in.

This advance put the German panzers only 19 km (12 miles) to the south of Prokhorovka and not too far from Rotmistrov's left flank. Clearly they would be a threat if they were to attack in support of the SS panzers. Rotmistrov detached half of his reserves – a tank brigade and three infantry brigades – under his deputy General Kuzma Trufanov. He sent this force to block the route that the III Panzer Corps would need to take should it seek to interfere.

Rotmistrov planned to use the 5th Guards Tank Army to launch a frontal assault on the SS panzers, while the 5th Guards Army was to march south to cut off the German retreat. The SS Totenkopf Division in the north with its 122 tanks and assault guns was to be held by a relatively weak attack composed mostly of infantry and artillery. A strong force of tanks from the 170th and 181st Tank Brigades was to destroy the bridges over the River Psel so that the Totenkopf could not cross over to join the main tank battle. The hope was to pin down the Totenkopf while it was surrounded and cut off by movements elsewhere.

The central SS Leibstandarte Division of 77 tanks and assault guns was to be hit by the strongest elements in the Soviet attack. More than 400 tanks and assault guns were to launch the offensive designed to break through and pulverize the German forces.

In the south SS Das Reich with 95 tanks and assault guns was to be attacked by over 100 tanks and assault guns. All the Soviet tank forces had large infantry support units to accompany them into battle.

Rotmistrov held back in reserve, under his personal command, 113 tanks plus supporting infantry and artillery.

In his orders issued in preparation for the attack to come, Rotmistrov told his men, 'Victory against the Tigers and Elefants can be achieved only by close action fighting. The T-34s must take maximum advantage of their great speed and tighter turning circles to achieve flanking fire against the side armour and rear armour of the German vehicles where they are most vulnerable.' It was good advice so far as it went, but Rotmistrov failed to mention the greater range of the German guns and their fatal hitting power.

The first indication that Hausser had that anything was wrong came at 6 am when he received a report from SS Leibstandarte headquarters that their forward patrols were hearing the sounds of large numbers of tank engines. There were not supposed to be any large concentrations of Soviet armour for several kilometres around. At 6.30 am the German air force arrived to pound the Soviet defensive positions previously scouted. From a high level, bombers dropped their loads over a wider area, while Stukas went down to pound individual strongpoints with greater accuracy. As the aircraft flew away, at 6.50 am, the German attack began as planned when elements of the SS Leibstandarte launched an attack against Soviet infantry holding the village of Storozhevoe. The Soviets fell back after a short struggle.

'Steel, steel, steel'

At 8 am a sudden Soviet artillery barrage began. The heavy shells thundered down around the Germans for half an hour, then the bombardment stopped as suddenly as it had started. Rotmistrov pressed the transmit button on his command radio and gave the codewords 'Steel, steel, steel'. It was the order for his attack to begin. Moments later a mass of purple flares went up into the sky, fired by the forward German patrols. It was the standard signal to warn of a Soviet armoured advance. The number of flares and their position showed that large Soviet forces were on the move.

Surging forwards against SS Leibstandarte came 500 tanks and self-propelled guns. One of the first German units into action was a company of seven Panzer IVs commanded by Major Rudolf von Ribbentrop, son of the German Foreign Minister Joachim von Ribbentrop. Major von Ribbentrop later recalled: 'We reached the crest of a hill. Ahead of us was another hill on the other side of a small valley about 200 metres wide on which our infantry were positioned. This small valley ran to our left and we drove down into it. I looked up the hill to my left and saw the first T-34s apparently trying to outflank us. About 150–200 metres from me over the crest appeared fifteen, then thirty, then forty tanks. Finally there were too many of them to count. The avalanche of enemy tanks came straight at us. Tank after tank, formation after formation. It was an unbelievable mass of tanks, and moving at a faster speed that I ever saw before.'

As previously in tank attacks, the Soviets sought to get to close quarters as quickly as they could. The Soviet tanks kept moving, even firing while on the move, adopting swift turning movements and sweeping curves to try to put the German gunners off their aim. Ribbentrop's panzers soon found themselves surrounded by a horde of fast-moving enemy tanks. After exchanging fire for some minutes, Ribbentrop decided that he was too heavily outnumbered and drove his tanks as fast as he could away from the fighting, then turned west to close up with his division's main body.

The determination of the T-34 crews to get to close quarters produced scenes of mayhem and confusion. Hundreds of tanks were wheeling, firing and burning in a compact area of open steppe. At ranges of 100 metres (330 feet) or less the tanks blasted at each other, expending ammunition at an unprecedented rate.

Ribbentrop described some of the combat. 'We stopped 10 m from a T-34 and fired. We made a direct hit on the Russian turret. The T-34 exploded in a sheet of flame. Its turret flew high into the air, then crashed down almost hitting us. I saw burning T-34 tanks continuing to run after being hit, colliding with each other in the confused space. It was an inferno of smoke, fire and exploding shells. T-34s burned. Men ran and crawled to escape the flames.'

Michael Wittmann, the much-admired Tiger commander of the SS Leibstandarte, was bringing his four Tigers up to join the battle when he saw a mass of T-34s coming towards him. These were the tanks sent by Rotmistrov to destroy the bridges over the Psel and isolate the SS Totenkopf from the other SS divisions. Wittmann moved his tanks into a fold in the ground to enable him to take the Soviets in the flank as they passed by.

Then, at a range of 1,000 metres (3,300 feet), Wittmann opened fire, destroying several T-34s before the Soviets could locate the source of the fire. Once they spotted the Tigers they swung away from the Psel and instead raced towards the Tigers, adopting their usual tactic of firing on the run in the hope of getting behind the Tigers to hit their less thick rear armour. Wittmann began to move, stopping to fire every few minutes.

Soon the Tigers were engulfed in a whirling mass of Soviet tanks, all vehicles moving at high speed for a tank combat. At one point a T-34 was hit and set on fire by a Tiger, but continued moving and ran headlong into Wittmann's tank. Wittmann's driver slammed the Tiger into reverse and powered away just seconds before the T-34 exploded in a ball of flame as its ammunition was set off by the fire. The Soviet tanks were driven off, then returned. For more than three hours, Wittmann and his Tigers battled the T-34s in a fast-moving struggle that ranged for large distances over the steppes.

It was not just the tanks that were involved: panzergrenadiers and Soviet infantry were also fighting. Both sets of infantry were trained to attack tanks, and sought to do so when they could, but they also battled each other. By mid morning the Germans were getting their anti-tank guns into operation.

Communicating with their tanks by radio, the gun commanders began to provide a degree of stability to the fighting. The guns were positioned into folds of the land where they were not immediately noticeable. The German tanks then began to manoeuvre into positions so that as the Soviet tanks raced towards them they came into range of the anti-tank guns. Taking advantage of the poor visibility of the Soviet tankmen, the Germans opened fire without being seen.

As the fight became less fluid and more structured, the Soviet losses mounted. No longer able to swarm around the German tanks, the Soviets found their preferred tactics being cramped and squeezed out. The panzergrenadiers likewise began to take up more usual positions and tactics, working in co-operation with the tanks and anti-tank guns.

German mastery of the sky

As the battle on the ground began to become more structured, to the advantage of the Germans, the low, dense cloud that had effectively stopped aircraft from taking a hand cleared. Around 1 pm aircraft began to appear over the battlefield. By this stage the Soviets had the advantage in terms of numbers of aircraft in the air, but the qualitative advantage was with the Germans, meaning that the aerial combats were finely balanced.

What made the real difference in the vast tank battle taking place south-west of Prokhorovka was the decision of Rotmistrov to concentrate his air power on the III Panzer Corps to the south and the XLVIII Panzer Corps to the west. The inevitable result was that over the developing tank battle the Germans swiftly gained mastery.

Adding to the hitting power of the Luftwaffe was the deployment of two new aircraft types. Both were upgrades of aircraft already in operation, especially tailored to destroy tanks. The B-2 Rüstsatz was a new version of the already effective ground attack HS129. In addition to the bombs and machine-guns, the B-2 Rütsatz variant mounted a MK103 cannon in an underslung pod fixed to the fuselage. This 30 mm cannon had a high rate of fire at 380 rounds per minute and a belt feed to ensure an adequate supply of ammunition. The cannon was made of lightweight materials to make it better suited to use in an aircraft, helping to improve the HS129 performance.

The second new aircraft over Prokhorovka was the G-2 Stuka. This variant had a more powerful Jumo 211J engine, allowing the Stuka to be given armour plating around the crew and engine for the first time. For weaponry the G-2 had a pair of 37 mm cannon, one under each wing. These guns were the Bordkanone BK37, which had a high muzzle velocity that helped with armour penetration, and could fire at 160 rounds per minute.

The BK37 cannon fired a specially designed armour-piercing round that had a core of solid tungsten-carbide steel. This revolutionary round produced what was to become known as a 'kinetic energy penetrator'. The outer, lightweight jacket and wide base allowed the gun to produce a very high muzzle velocity using only a small propellant charge that in turn gave a small recoil, making this ideal for an aircraft. When the round struck tank armour the outer jacket fell off, leaving the narrow, long tungsten-carbide core to concentrate all the force of its weight and speed on a very small area of armour. The round was therefore able to penetrate the armour, spraying the inside of the tank with lethal, razor-sharp fragments of armour as well as ricocheting around the interior itself. This revolutionary round proved to be murderously effective and was later to be adopted by all armies.

Shifting fortunes

As the skies cleared, the German aircraft swooped down to attack the Soviet tanks. Casualties mounted, but the Soviets pressed forward with undiminished enthusiasm. An elevation the Germans had codenamed Hill 252.2 dominated the centre of the battlefield and at about noon was captured by Soviet infantry, recaptured an hour later by panzergrenadiers and retaken by the Soviets around 3 pm, then fell back into German hands in the early evening.

While this vast tank battle was taking place in the centre, the SS Totenkopf had launched its own attack at dawn as planned. Moving along the north bank of the River Psel the SS Totenkopf found itself facing Soviet infantry, backed by anti-tank guns and a handful of tanks. The Soviet defences had been hurriedly constructed and were nothing like as strong those that had been overcome in the earlier fighting.

By 1 pm the SS Totenkopf had captured another significant hill (codenamed 226.6) and were well on their way to reaching the point where they planned to turn south to attack the Soviet defences around Prokhorovka from the northern flank. They were then struck by a counter-attack launched by the fresh units of the 5th Guards Army. By this point the SS Totenkopf was well aware of the vast tank force attacking SS Leibstandarte. Now struck by a major counteroffensive of their own, the SS Totenkopf's advance ground to a halt. Their commander, Hermann Priess, had no wish to see his unit cut off and so halted his advance until the position became clearer.

SS Das Reich was meantime hit by another Soviet offensive. This attack was led by infantry, supported by a long-range heavy-artillery bombardment and self-propelled guns. The attack was pushed forwards with great courage and determination, and brought the SS Das Reich to a halt.

The III Panzer Corps at Rzhavets had meanwhile moved its main strength over the Donets and sorted itself after the savage night battle. Learning of the vast tank battle engulfing the SS corps, Breith ordered his panzers north to lend support. The 19th Panzer Division led the way, with 20 Tigers forming the spearhead of the assault. Rotmistrov was informed of the move and sent his reserves to block the III Panzer Corps.

At 4 pm the SS Leibstandarte moved over to the attack for the first time since the horde of Soviet tanks had first appeared. The weather chose this moment to break, with violent thunderstorms moving across the battlefield and denying the skies to the Luftwaffe ground-attack aircraft. As the SS tanks pushed forwards they encountered the usual mix of anti-tank guns and infantry, but were fighting their way through slowly. Then a fresh mass of 120 Soviet tanks roared out of the rain and an entirely new tank battle erupted. The Soviets were driven off after some hours of combat, but by then dusk was drawing in.

Nightfall found the Das Reich stationary and similarly continuing to fight off Soviet assaults led by infantry and supported by tanks. The III Panzer Corps was meanwhile still inching north against ferocious Soviet resistance.

The great tank battle of Prokhorovka was over.

Cost of combat

The II SS Panzer Corps had lost 842 men killed or wounded during the day. The loss in tanks and assault guns had been

T-34

This medium tank could be equated to the Panzer IV. It weighed 26 tonnes, was armed with a 76 mm gun plus two machine-guns and could reach more than 50 km/h (30 mph) on roads. Its wide tracks made it suitable for use on soft soil while its sloped armour made it proof against many German anti-tank weapons.

Although of good design, the T-34 had its drawbacks. The small turret meant that there was space for only two men, requiring the commander also to fire the gun, which rather hampered his concentration. He was also hampered by the fact that his seat did not turn with the turret, but remained fixed to the chassis floor. The lack of a radio made it impossible for orders to be sent to a tank once it was in action, or for tank commanders to co-operate in combat. Just as bad was the propensity of the tracks to fall apart on roads or frozen ground.

In line with Stalin's dictum about boosting production of weaponry, the T-34 was designed with mass production in mind. It was crudely designed and crudely built, allowing huge numbers to roll off the assembly lines. To further boost numbers, there was only one type of T-34 – in contrast to most other countries, which produced a number of variants of each model for different purposes. This led to some problems on the battlefield and held back improvements to the basic design as time passed.

By 1943 the T-34 was becoming outclassed. More recent models of the Panzer IV had armour proof against the Soviet gun, while the Tiger and Panther could knock out T-34s with ease.

A Jagdpanzer IV, a tank destroyer armed with a 75mm Pak42 gun mounted on the chassis of a Panzer IV. The weapon was rushed into production after the summer battles of 1942 to counter the Soviet T-34 but it proved to be front-heavy and unstable on rough terrain.

After Kursk the T-34 underwent a major redesign in an effort to make it capable of taking on the new generation of panzers. The turret was enlarged to enable it to mount the 85 mm 52K gun. The turret could also hold a third man, allowing the commander to concentrate fully on commanding the tank for the first time as there was now room for a gunner. This new T-34-85 outclassed the new models of Panzer IV, but was still no match for the Tiger or Panther.

The T-34-85 remained the main battle tank of the Red Army until the mid 1950s and was produced until 1958. Other variants of the T-34 were in production until 1969. In all 35,120 T-34 and 48,950 T-34-85 tanks were built.

When the T-34 finally became obsolete, the Soviet Union began exporting the model to communist governments around the world. Although obsolete in the context of a Soviet/US conflict, the tanks remained valuable military hardware in the developing world. In 2015 the T-34 was in service in more than a dozen countries, such as Angola, Mozambique and Zimbabwe.

Tiger Tank

The Tiger tank that fought at Kursk was the Panzer Mk VI Tiger Ausf E, usually called the Tiger I. In 1944 it would be replaced by the Tiger II, sometimes called the King Tiger.

The Tiger I was a revolutionary weapon. It was massively heavy with extremely thick armour, but its powerful engine and wide tracks meant that its performance was equal to that of many tanks less than half its weight. The Germans had been toying with the idea of a heavy tank for some years, but it was the experience of fighting the T-34 that convinced the high command to back one. It was rushed into production, with the unfortunate effect that some teething problems were experienced in combat. The Tiger was designed to be a type of land battleship. It had armour thick enough to make it invulnerable to incoming fire, while it was armed with a gun powerful enough to knock out any enemy tanks.

When it entered service, the Tiger was the most powerful weapon on the battlefield. At Kursk the Soviets had no real answer to the Tiger, their tanks suffering massive losses to it. Later the Allies produced tanks that could disable a Tiger from the side or rear, but head-on the Tiger remained supreme. The most famous feat of the Tiger came in the Battle of Villers-Bocage on 13 June 1944 in Normandy when Michael Wittmann destroyed 14 British tanks and 17 other armoured vehicles in less than 20 minutes.

The front view of a Tiger I. The awesomely powerful 88mm KwK gun could destroy any tank in the world.

In 1944 production of the Tiger I ceased and that of the Tiger II began. The new Tiger had sloped armour and a rounded turret to make the armour more resistant to the more powerful Allied guns introduced to deal with the Tiger I. The new variant was so powerful that it was almost invulnerable on the field of battle. However, it suffered from a number of engine and mechanical problems that meant it broke down often enough to be of questionable value given its massive cost. In all 1,347 Tiger I tanks were built along with 492 Tiger IIs.

43 in all, but many of these had been only superficially damaged. Within a week all but two had been repaired and were back in the line. Of particular concern had been the fact that no less than 10 of the 15 Tigers had been put out of action, mostly due to damage to tracks. Although all 10 were soon back in operation there was concern. The enormous weight of the Tiger made it difficult to tow a damaged tank off the field to take to a makeshift repair workshop. The Germans held the battlefield at the close of day and so could repair the Tigers where they stood, but if they had been forced to retreat the Tigers would have been lost. The Luftwaffe reported that having flown 600 sorties that day, they had suffered 11 aircraft damaged, of which six were incapable of repair.

Compared to the German losses, the Soviets' were vast. The 5th Guards Tank Army had lost 7,600 men killed or wounded plus an astonishing 600 tanks and self-propelled guns lost, plus another 240 support vehicles destroyed. In other words, Rotmistrov had lost about three-quarters of his armoured vehicles in around 12 hours of combat.

When Stalin saw the figures, he phoned Rotmistrov to demand an explanation. 'Where is your army?' Stalin snarled down the line.

Deciding that Vatutin was not up to the job, Stalin sent Zhukov to take personal charge of the southern flank of the Kursk salient and prevent a final German breakthrough.

But, although nobody realized it, the crisis was over.

Chapter 9

NOISES OFF

While the fighting raging around Kursk had been absorbing the full attention of Hitler, Stalin and their senior commanders, the war had been continuing elsewhere with undiminished fury.

In the Pacific theatre, the Japanese were reeling from their catastrophic defeat the previous year at the naval Battle of Midway. As yet the Allies lacked the resources to take the offensive in a major way, but were on the advance on New Guinea and the Solomon Islands. In China a stalemate had set in, with neither the Japanese nor Chinese having the strength to launch any major offensives. In Burma the British had just failed in an effort to advance down the Arakan Peninsula, and the Japanese were considering an invasion of India by way of Kohima and Imphal.

In the Atlantic the convoy war had reached its climax. So many Allied merchant ships had been sunk in the first six months of the year that food was running low, and fuel was dangerously low. There was a real concern that unless things improved before the onset of winter there might be widespread hunger and deaths from cold in Britain. June had seen major changes in the Battle of the Atlantic as the Allies introduced new weapons, new radar and more escort vessels. It was starting to look as if the Allies might be winning the campaign.

Allies edging towards victory

The crucial theatre, however, turned out to be what many considered to be a war area of only secondary importance: the Mediterranean. Since the outbreak of war a major naval campaign had raged between the British Royal Navy and Italian Regia Marina. This had at times had been finely balanced, but now tilted heavily in favour of Britain. A land campaign in North Africa had seen the Italo-German forces under Erwin Rommel deep inside Egypt and poised to overrun that country, seize the Suez Canal and sweep on to capture the vital oil fields beyond; that campaign had now ended with a decisive Allied victory and no Axis forces remained in North Africa.

The big question occupying planners on both sides in the Mediterranean was what the Allies would do next. Hitler had poured resources into the war against Russia, so his commanders in the Mediterranean – Erwin Rommel and Albert Kesselring – clearly could not take the offensive. The Allies, however, had three options open to them. They could launch an invasion of Greece, which had been under joint Italo-German occupation since 1941. They could invade Sicily, an integral part of Italy, a key ally of Germany. Or they could land troops in southern France to begin the liberation of that country.

Operation Mincemeat

On 30 April 1943 the Spanish coast guard had found the body of a British officer washed up on a beach at Punta Umbria. The body appeared to have come from an aircraft crash and had chained to its wrist a sealed document briefcase. Inside the briefcase the Spanish found a collection of top-secret British Army documents. These included details of promotions and sackings, discussion of disputes between British and American servicemen and letters between senior commanders. The key document, however, was a report being sent to Sir Harold Alexander, commander of the 18th Army Group in North Africa, which outlined the role his troops were to play in the invasion of Greece that was to take place in late July.

The Spanish gave the officer a proper military burial, then passed the documents on to the Germans. At this date Spanish dictator Francisco Franco was seeking to stay on friendly terms with Hitler, who appeared to be winning the war; but he had no intention of actually joining the conflict as Hitler hoped. Handing over top-secret documents would help curry favour with the German government.

The Germans studied the documents and concluded that the threat to Greece was real and imminent. They moved several troop units to Greece to bolster the defences there, and even moved Rommel to the area.

In fact the documents were all fakes produced by British intelligence. The 'dead officer' was the body of a Welsh tramp who had died a few weeks earlier and whose body had been kept chilled ready to be used. It had been dumped off the Spanish beach by a British submarine, which also unloaded into the sea various bits of wreckage that might be expected from an air crash. The ruse – Operation Mincemeat – had been developed to try to convince the Germans that the Allies were about to invade Greece, when in fact they were going to attack Sicily.

Battle for Sicily

The invasion of Sicily duly went ahead in the early hours of 10 July 1943. The invasion was a highly complex affair involving British, American and Canadian armies, plus ships and aircraft from all three nations. Some troops landed from boats, some floated down on parachutes. Bombers pounded defences while naval ships laid down a barrage or patrolled offshore to stop the Italian navy interfering. It was a huge operation involving 160,000 men, hundreds of ships and a vast aerial armada. The defending forces comprised 230,000 Italian troops and 40,000 Germans.

The Allied landings of Sicily did not go well, largely due to a sudden storm that blew up. Landing craft were driven off course and paratroops landed a long way from their targets. The defenders reacted quickly and moved to stop the invaders from seizing key airfields and high ground. By the end of the first day of the invasion it was unclear whether or not the Allies would be able to secure a firm foothold on Sicily.

On 11 July, the second day of the Sicily landings, the Axis scored some notable victories. A British landing at Augusta was driven back into the sea while American efforts to capture three airfields were likewise thwarted with heavy losses. The following day a counter-attack by Italian tanks smashed the British Wiltshire Regiment before being halted by anti-tank guns. That same day another Italian unit successfully blocked the American advance toward Canicatii.

By nightfall on 12 July, the day of the vast tank battle around Prokhorovka, it seemed as if the Allied landings in

Sicily might be in trouble. On the other hand Hitler knew that the Italian people were fed up with the ever-growing length of what Mussolini had promised them would be a short war. Italian industrialists were deeply disturbed by the cost of the war, in terms of both what it was costing the government in cash and what it was costing them through lost trade. Even elements within Mussolini's own Fascist government were disillusioned and looking for a way out.

Hitler had read the assessments of his diplomats and knew that there was a real chance of some sort of coup against Mussolini if Italy were to suffer a serious blow. The loss of Italian colonies in Africa had undermined Mussolini's position. The loss of Sicily would fatally weaken it. If Sicily fell, Hitler knew, the chances were that Mussolini would fall soon after. If that happened then the new Italian government would almost certainly make peace with the Allies.

Quagmire on the Eastern Front

The fighting in Sicily was for very high stakes indeed. So far, however, it was inconclusive. Although it was a serious distraction for Hitler, his main focus remained the Eastern Front and in particular the fighting around Kursk.

The night after the savage tank battles around Prokhorovka the rain came down in torrents. The land over which the battles of the previous days had been fought were already churned by the passage of thousands of wheeled and tracked vehicles. The sudden downpour reduced the fields to mud and the gravel tracks to gloopy morass. The difficulties this caused for the trucks bringing up supplies and ammunition affected the

Germans worse than the Soviets for the most badly churned ground lay in the German rear.

Nevertheless, Manstein insisted that the offensive was to continue. The Soviet losses on the 12 July had been immense, and Manstein viewed the reckless Soviet attacks as evidence that the enemy was running out of options. Once again the II SS Panzer Corps was ordered to attack.

The SS advance did not get very far. Rotmistrov may have lost most of his armour, but still had large numbers of artillery and infantry of the 5th Guards Army. These were dug into defensive positions and their front liberally scattered with mines. By mid morning the exhausted SS units could advance no further. Rotmistrov then tried a counter-attack but that, too, proved to be a failure.

The III Panzer Corps of Army Detachment Kempf was meanwhile seeking to advance from its forward positions at Rzhavets in order to link up with SS Das Reich. The attack began well, and had only 8 km (5 miles) to go when it was brought to a halt by concentrated Soviet artillery fire on a massive scale.

Operation Kutuzov

Events on the northern flank of the Kursk salient had taken a far worse turn for the Germans. As a rule of thumb, Stalin always preferred attack to defence. It had taken all Zhukov's powers of persuasion to convince Stalin to stand on the defensive in the spring and summer of 1943 awaiting the German attack at Kursk that could be halted on massive defences.

That did not mean that the Soviets had no plans for offensive action in 1943, only that they had decided to wait until the Germans were exhausted after their own offensive before launching them. The site for the planned Soviet offensive was Oryol, north of Kursk.

German engineer troops prepare to assemble a prefabricated bridge under the watchful guns of a pair of Tiger tanks. Engineer battalions were essential to ensure the tanks could cross the many rivers and streams of the Eastern Front.

Just as there was a deep bulge into the German lines around Kursk, offering apparently vulnerable flanks to attack, so there was a deep bulge into Soviet lines around Oryol. The bulge was filled by the German 2nd Army and other elements of Army Group Centre that had not attacked at Kursk. These were almost exclusively infantry divisions since all the panzers and self-propelled guns had been transferred to Model's 9th Army for the assault. There may have been almost a quarter of a million men in the Oryol salient, but without tanks or assault guns they were vulnerable.

Making the idea of an attack at Oryol even more attractive to the Soviets was the prospect of the German attack at Kursk. They calculated, correctly, that the Germans would commit most of their armour to the Kursk offensive. That meant that the Germans would be launching an attack heading south from the Oryol Salient. If the Soviets successfully attacked to Oryol while that thrust was stuck deep in the Kursk Salient a major part of the German panzer force could be cut off, surrounded and destroyed.

The area around Oryol had been held by the Germans for more than a year. While German military doctrine emphasized the importance of movement and panzer firepower in defeating the Soviets, the German soldiers were only human. They had therefore constructed a mass of semi-permanent huts and dugouts to make their lives more comfortable and give protection from the blistering heat of summer and bitter cold of winter. These structures were protected against partisan attack by networks of barbed wire, trenches and minefields. While these defences were on nothing like the scale of the Soviet preparations around Kursk, they were not inconsiderable obstacles.

Soviet staff officers had been working on the plans for an attack on Oryol since February. The operation was code-named Operation Kutuzov, paying homage to Mikhail Kutuzov, the Russian field marshal who had fought Napoleon to a standstill at Borodino in 1812, then chased the French out of Russia.

During planning at the Stavka in February and March, the Soviets developed a plan that would see fast-moving columns of tanks and motorized infantry break through German lines at Kozelsk. Once through the German front lines the columns would head south at speed to reach the Soviet positions west of Kursk. This thrust would cut off the entire German 9th Army and most of the 2nd Army. If the newly established corridor could be held as firmly as had the corridor around Stalingrad the previous winter, the German losses would be immense.

In April the Stavka summoned the army commanders who would be undertaking the operation to a conference, which was also attended by Stalin. The key commanders were Ivan Bagramyan of the 11th Guards Army and Vasily Badanov of the 4th Tank Army. Together these two men would command the main thrust. As the Stavka staff officers outlined their plans, Bagramyan became increasingly alarmed.

When it was his turn to speak, Bagramyan protested that his forces were nowhere near strong enough for the task given to them. They could support the 4th Tank Army in an offensive, but not seal off the pocket and trap the

Germans. Bagramyan suggested instead that a less daring and ambitious plan be drawn up that would see a series of smaller attacks launched across the northern edge of the Oryol salient. He argued that launching a series of attacks at different points would unbalance the Germans and keep them guessing. In this way the Oryol salient could be pinched out. If the gains would not be so great, neither would the risks.

After the discussion had continued for some time, Stalin intervened. He suggested a compromise. A major thrust down the rear of the salient would be carried out by Bagramyan and Badanov. However, a series of smaller destabilizing attacks would also be carried out along the north-eastern shoulder of the salient by the 61st and 3rd Armies. The commanders were given until 24 May to get everything ready. Even before 24 May arrived, the Stavka issued orders that the offensive was to be delayed until after the expected German attack took place. The Soviets around Oryol settled down to wait.

While they waited, the German intelligence services became aware that they were there. Although the Germans underestimated the number of Soviets gathering to the north of Oryol they realized that a very substantial force was present. The commander of Army Group Center, von Kluge, began to get restive. He told the Commander of his 2nd Army, Walter Weiss, to prepare to defend against a major attack. Weiss in turn prepared his seven infantry divisions, but the force was spread thinly across a large area and was unavoidably weak.

To Weiss's north was the 4th Army, which was under the temporary command of General Hans von Salmuth while its real commander, Gotthard Heinrici, was away on leave. The absence of Heinrici was unfortunate for the Germans as he was one of the most skilled commanders of defence in the war. Among his tactics was to build defensive positions in full view of the enemy and ostentatiously man them before evacuating them just hours before an expected assault. In this way the Soviets expended vast amounts of artillery ammunition on the empty works and inflicted no casualties at all on the German defenders.

On 12 July, the same day as the SS panzers were fighting their epic tank battle around Prokhorovka to the south, a massive Soviet artillery bombardment opened up along the northern face of the Oryol salient. The bombardment was followed by a ground offensive in overwhelming force. The 11th Guards Army moved forward with six divisions on a 16-km (10-mile) front, on which the Germans had positioned only two infantry regiments. The Germans gave way and by dusk the 11th Guards had advanced 25 km (15 miles). Further east the Soviet attacks were less heavy and less successful, though even so they managed to advance roughly 10 km (6 miles) into the salient.

Von Kluge had been expecting an attack of some kind for weeks and was ready. Careful advance staff work had prepared transport to move troops and equipment to any threatened area of the Oryol salient. By the afternoon of 13 July, the second day of the Soviet attack, the 5th Panzer Division had been moved from a reserve position behind Model's attack towards Kursk to face the rapidly advancing 11th Guards Army. At first the panzers halted the Soviet advance, but then the 5th Tank Army came up and once again the Germans began to fall back, though much more slowly.

Soviet anti-tank guns dug into camouflaged positions near Oryol in July 1943. The Soviets often sought to lure German panzers forward to come within range of such hidden weaponry before opening fire.

German withdrawal

It was at this point, on the late afternoon of 13 July, that von Kluge and Manstein were summoned to the Wolf's Lair for a meeting with Hitler. When they arrived, they found that Hitler was in a highly excited state – even forgetting his usual role as jovial host that would have normally seen him offering refreshments to those who came to see him. Hitler treated his two senior commanders to a rant about the situation in Sicily and the weaknesses of the Italian government that amounted almost to a monologue.

Hitler then turned to the situation on the Eastern Front. If Manstein and von Kluge thought they were going to be able to get a word in, they were wrong. Hitler read out extracts from various reports on the situation and intelligence of Soviet strengths and intentions. He then abruptly turned back to Italy and announced that reinforcements were needed there to forestall Allied landings on the Italian mainland.

'I have nothing more I can withdraw from anywhere else, so the reinforcements must come from the Kursk Front. I am therefore forced to cancel *Zitadelle*.'

Von Kluge was at last able to speak. He asked if this meant that he could withdraw Model's units from their advanced positions in order to face the Soviets attacking the Oryol salient. On being told that it did, von Kluge fell silent, presumably working out in his head what he was going to do with Model's troops.

Manstein then spoke. He emphasized the staggering losses that the Soviets had suffered in the last few days. He also pointed out that his troops were now north of the fortified belt of Soviet defences and into more open country that favoured the Germans. He asked for a delay of several days so that he could continue to inflict heavy losses. He held out the prospect that by destroying huge quantities of Soviet armour he could forestall any major Soviet offensive for the rest of the summer.

After thinking for some time, Hitler nodded. Manstein could have his battle.

Chapter 10

OPERATION ROLAND

Even before leaving his meeting with Hitler on 13 July, Manstein had phoned his own headquarters to tell them to start planning what became Operation Roland. This was a last-ditch effort to smash and cripple the Soviet forces in southern Russia and so stop the Soviets from launching an offensive that year.

Manstein's staff planned to use the salient gained by the II SS Panzer Corps as an anvil against which the XXIV Panzer Corps and III Panzer Corps would act as a hammer to smash the Soviets. The XXIV Panzer Corps had played little part in the offensive to date. Manstein had been holding it back in reserve.

When he got back to his headquarters late that night, however, he found that while he had been travelling an order had arrived from Hitler. Manstein never found out why Hitler had changed his mind, or who had been talking to him, but the XXIV Panzer Corps was being moved out of Manstein's command area and sent south to boost the forces of von Mackensen's 1st Panzer Army along the River Dnieper.

Deprived of his only real reinforcements, Manstein recast the plans for Operation Roland with what he had. Now the II SS Panzer Corps and III Panzer Corps were to link up as soon as they could, while the reasonably fresh 167th and 168th Infantry Divisions would attack the Soviet forces thus caught in a pocket and eliminate them. This should provoke a large-scale Soviet counter offensive over the open steppes that could be defeated with crushing losses as had the attack at Prokhorovka a few days earlier.

Manstein's initial success

The Roland offensive began at dawn on 14 July with an artillery bombardment along the entire front held by the II SS Panzer Corps. Along much of the length it was a feint, designed to keep the Soviet forces where they were. Only the SS Das Reich Division moved, lunging forward to strike south-east. The attack was led by panzergrenadiers, with the panzers coming up in support. When the Soviets launched an armoured counter-attack it led only to serious Soviet tank losses. Manstein's plan seemed to be working.

The III Panzer Corps was meanwhile was fighting its way north. The Soviet troops that were likely to be caught in the pocket when the two panzer forces met were already on the move, heading north-east to get out of the trap.

Zhukov himself arrived at the front that day. He listened to the commanders on the spot and studied the forces available. He concluded that the Soviet strategy of the previous days would continue. The Soviets would continue to feed in vast reserves of men, tanks and artillery in order to entangle the panzers in slow, stationary battles where they could not take advantage of their superior speed and manoeuvrability. The German panzer forces were to be ground down with massive losses of Soviet lives and Soviet equipment as the price to be paid.

Next day, 15 July, the SS Das Reich and III Panzer Corps finally linked up. Manstein had been planning at this point to turn his tanks east and strike across the open land south of Prokhorovka. This armoured thrust across open ground would be bound to provoke a Soviet response, allowing Manstein to inflict heavy casualties. But without the XXIV Panzer Corps, he had only the tired forces that had already been fighting a gruelling battle for ten days.

Short on fuel, ammunition, spare parts and lubricants, the panzers could not move. The Soviets began launching a series of small-scale attacks, co-ordinated with each other so that if the local German reserves went to bolster one danger point they would arrive to find the attack slackening while a new assault was being launched elsewhere. This gruelling ploy was being used to wear out German vehicles with fruitless journeys back and forth across the battlefield.

On 17 July, Manstein finally gave up. He ordered his troops to stand and hold the ground they had captured while his staff worked out a way to extricate them from their exposed positions with minimal risk.

Soviets' power in numbers

Operation Kutuzov, meanwhile, had been proceeding around Oryol. On 16 July the Soviets widened their offensive as the smaller-scale attacks on the eastern face of the Oryol salient gained in power and ferocity. The Soviets now had 1.3 million men in action, with 2,400 tanks and 23,000 guns. The Germans were aghast at the sheer scale of the forces bearing down on them, unable to believe that the Soviets could put such forces into the field. The Germans themselves could muster only 300,000 men, 600 tanks and 5,500 guns.

Despite the vast disparity in numbers the fighting was not going entirely the way that the Soviets wanted. Their casualties were larger than they had expected and their advance slower.

Model now sent all his armour north as fast as he could to bolster the German defences. His infantry followed more slowly, reluctantly giving up the ground that they had fought so hard to conquer. The Soviets followed them step by step, launching minor attacks if the German retreat looked likely to halt. In truth they did not want to hurry the withdrawal of the 9th Army from the Kursk salient. If the 9th Army lingered, then there was all the more chance that the Soviet Oryol offensive would trap it and allow it to be annihilated as had the 6th Army at Stalingrad. By 18 July the 9th Army was back where it had been before the Kursk Offensive had begun.

Four days later the German retreat picked up pace. The 9th Army was now out of danger of being cut off and could fall back west towards Bryansk. This greatly shortened the length of the front line, allowing the Germans to thicken their forces and make defence a more realistic option. Even so, the retreat went on. Oryol itself fell on 4 August and two weeks later the Soviets were approaching Bryansk.

When he learned of the damage inflicted on his beloved panzer units, Heinz Guderian was shocked and depressed. He ordered that all the units be taken out of the front line so that their battered vehicles could be subjected to a thorough overhaul and maintenance schedule, while vehicles that had been irretrievably lost had to be replaced. Having given these orders, Guderian then collapsed. For some time he had been ignoring pains in his stomach, but now the blow he felt at the terrible damage to the panzers seemed to hit him as hard physically as it had psychologically.

A move against Hitler?

Within days Guderian was laid up in hospital and quite unable to work while he awaited surgery. That did not stop him getting a visit from General Henning von Tresckow. Von Tresckow came from a high-class Prussian military family and was linked by family, marriage and friendship to many of the most senior army officers and industrialists in Germany. When he visited Guderian, he broached a difficult issue.

Hitler, von Tresckow said, was proving to be a liability in military matters. He interfered with the generals, refused to listen to what his advisors told him and made disastrous decisions. After all, it had been Hitler who had authorized *Zitadelle* and so destroyed the panzer forces. Guderian listened, but when von Tresckow moved on to his suggestion as to what to do about the situation, Guderian blanched.

'We need to reduce Hitler's powers as Supreme Commander,' suggested von Tresckow. It was a deliberately loosely worded phrase. It could be taken to mean simply that the regular chain of command should be restored by appointing a new head of

OKW and restoring Hitler to his proper role as head of government. That would put operational command of the armed forces back under the control of professional army officers. Guderian, however, thought that von Tresckow meant that they needed to organize a military coup to take over the government of Germany by force. He would have nothing to do with it.

Von Tresckow also contacted other senior officers at this time. Manstein sent him packing with the words 'Prussian officers do not mutiny', while von Kluge refused to do anything unless other senior commanders moved first. Finally von Tresckow gave up thoughts of reining in Hitler. Instead he moved on to plotting the assassination of Hitler, a process that would culminate in the 20 July bomb plot.

Peace in the west?

It was not only military officers who recognized what the defeat of *Zitadelle* really meant. Heinrich Himmler was one of the Nazi Party's oldest and most loyal members. He had joined as early as 1923, taking a role in propaganda, membership recruitment and party bureaucracy. In 1929 he became head of the SS, or *Schutzstaffel,* then a group of toughs who protected Nazi Party public meetings from disruption by political opponents. By means of adroitly denouncing rivals, making himself useful and pandering to Hitler's racial and political foibles, Himmler rose through the ranks. By 1943 he was in charge of the Gestapo and the SS (now a mini-army in its own right) and was super-

Pavel Rotmistrov (1901–82)

Rotmistrov was born in 1901 in a rural part of Tver, in western Russia. As a teenager he was an early and enthusiastic recruit to the Communist Party. He joined the Red Army in 1919 as an infantryman, achieving quick promotion to an officer. In 1921 he helped to put down the Krondstadt Rebellion, a key event that saw the death of Communist claims to reflect the wishes of the people and the imposition of a brutal dictatorship under Lenin.

In 1928 Rotmistrov became a staff officer and later served as a military instructor, training other officers. When the war broke out he was Chief of Staff to the 3rd Mechanized Corps, which was almost completely destroyed in less than three weeks by the German forces advancing on Leningrad. Rotmistrov escaped the disaster and served in a variety of staff posts before taking command of the 5th Guards Tank Army in February 1943.

After Kursk, Rotmistrov retained command of the 5th Guards Tank Army, but in July 1944 he again suffered massive losses during a rash attack on German forces at Minsk. This time he was relieved of his command and given a staff job. He never again held an active command, but instead filled a succession of staff and administrative posts in the armoured branch of the Red Army until his retirement in 1968.

Pavel Rotmistrov was commander of the 5th Guards Tank Army, and was largely responsible for its massive losses at Kursk.

vising the extermination of the Jews living within the Reich's territory.

Himmler had his agents inserted into every aspect of the German state. He knew the truth about weapons production, military recruitment and the ability of the German state to wage war. He recognized the defeat at Kursk for the catastrophe that it really was. It was immediately clear to Himmler that Germany could not win the war. Knowing that after the widespread outrages, murders and slaughters that the SS and other Germans had carried out in the east there was no chance of a negotiated peace with the Soviets, Himmler instead looked to the west. He calculated that the Western Powers might be willing to agree to a peace deal that gave them all their war aims in Western Europe on the grounds that this would free them to concentrate on the war against Japan.

Himmler turned to a neighbour named Carl Langbehn, a lawyer who had extensive foreign contacts. Intermediaries tested the water before Himmler met him at the end of August 1943. Langbehn then set off on a holiday to the neutral country of Switzerland, courtesy of a travel permit issued by Himmler. Once in Switzerland, Langbehn made contact with British diplomats to ask about a possible end to the war.

Unfortunately for Himmler, and disastrously for Langbehn, the British Embassy passed on the request to London by radio using a top-secret code system that had been broken by the Germans. The Nazi intelligence services intercepted the signal and decoded it. Langbehn was arrested on his return to

Germany and subjected to torture. Exactly what happened next is unclear, but Langbehn was handed over to the SS and promptly executed – presumably on the orders of Himmler who was trying to cover his tracks.

Also concerned by the turn of events was Hermann Goering, head of the Luftwaffe. Rather than seek to broker a peace deal, he began distancing himself from the more murderous activities of the Nazi regime and destroying evidence of his involvement. No doubt he was acting with an eye to explaining his actions to the victorious Allies when the war was over.

Meanwhile, the fighting went on.

Chapter 11

AFTERMATH

The Battle of Kursk had been designed by the Germans to annihilate the Soviet armies located in the large Kursk salient. In fact it had resulted in the destruction of the German panzer forces. The extent of the disaster was clear to certain top Nazis, but was hidden from even the most senior generals. They were lied to methodically by Hitler, who kept all sources of information in his own hands and revealed only what he wanted.

Nothing, however, could disguise the weakness of the German Army when the Soviets began to move forward after Kursk. In the north the Oryol salient was overrun in Operation Kutuzov. The Soviet attack in the south was slower to get going, but more significant. After the failure of the Kursk offensive, Manstein pulled his troops back to positions around Belgorod near where they had started their offensive.

In August the Soviets launched an offensive that put its main strength at the point where the 4th Panzer Army linked to Army Detachment Kempf. The joint was weak due to poor communications between the two forces, a problem exacerbated by the lack of panzers in the two units. The Soviets pierced the German defences, then turned sideways to widen the gap between the two German forces. Within a week the gap was more than 50 km (30 miles) wide.

Manstein wrote an appreciation of the situation. 'It is clear that no action by these forces, nor indeed by those of the Army Group as a whole, could provide a long-term answer to the Soviet attack. Our casualties are already alarmingly high and two divisions have broken down completely as a result of continuous overstrain. It is beyond any possible shadow of doubt the enemy is now resolved to force an issue against the German southern wing.'

Zeitzler flew out to see Manstein, who was in no mood to beat about the bush. He told Zeitzler that either he had to be given another ten divisions or he would have to abandon the entire Donets area, including the strategic city of Kharkov. Zeitzler took the message back to Hitler at OKH, but Manstein received neither the new divisions (which were not available) nor permission to retreat.

Germans in full retreat

Without the panzers and men lost at Kursk, Manstein could not hold out. His line cracked open and on 22 August Kharkov fell to the Soviets. Thereafter the German retreat was inexorable. There would be no further advances on the Eastern Front. The only direction of travel was westwards. The Soviet advances would at times be spasmodic as the Germans fought tenaciously for every inch of ground or as the Soviet advances outran their own supply system. But the retreat that began at Kharkov was constant until it ended at Berlin two years later.

Kharkov was the third-largest industrial city in the Soviet Union in 1941. During 1943 it changed hands three times, leaving little more than burned out ruins by the time it finally fell to the Soviets in August 1943.

Historians and military experts have long recognized that the defeat at Kursk marked the final chance that the Germans had of defeating Russia. After Kursk the Germans were quite unable to launch a large-scale offensive. The massive onslaughts of 1941 and 1942 were a thing of the past.

Whether or not Kursk was actually a chance for victory is a more finely balanced question. If the offensive had succeeded as planned, it would have resulted in colossal loss to the Soviet war machine at trifling cost to the Germans. Moreover the German panzer armies would have remained intact and ready for future offensives on an equally enormous scale.

However, the Soviets had absorbed punishment on a huge scale before and not been defeated. In the Battle of Kiev, fought in August 1941, they had lost more than 700,000 men in less than three weeks. At Minsk a few weeks earlier they had lost 350,000 men. In all 1941 saw the Red Army lose 4 million men. Yet by summer 1943 it was stronger than ever before. Stalin had been correct, the war would be decided on the factory floor. The brutal truth was that Germany could not defeat the Soviet Union.

Kursk proved that beyond all doubt.

Index

Picture Credits

Getty Images: 9 (ullstein bild); 23 (ullstein bild); 27 (ullstein bild); 41 (ullstein bild); 48 (Keystone); 53(Laski Diffusion); 59 (SVF2); 65 (Sovfoto/UIG); 85 (ullstein bild); 104 (Sovfoto); 128 (ullstein bild); 139 (Heritage Images); 153 (IWM); 155 (Interim Archives); 163 (ullstein bild); 168 (Heritage Images); 182 (Hulton Archive);

Mary Evans Picture Library: 21 (Sueddeutsche Zeitung Photo); 57 (picture alliance/ZB); 71 (SZ Photo/Scherl);

Rupert Matthews: 83; 89; 93; 101;

Topfoto: 177 (SCRSS)